NEW YORK ELEGIES

· ·

Ukrainian Studies

Series Editor

Vitaly Chernetsky (University of Kansas)

Other Titles in this Series:

Words for War: New Poems from Ukraine
Edited by Oksana Maksymchuk & Max Rosochinsky

*The White Chalk of Days: The Contemporary Ukrainian Literature
Series Anthology*
Compiled and edited by Mark Andryczyk

*From the Bible to Shakespeare: Pantelejmon Kuliš (1819–97) and the
Formation of Literary Ukrainian*
Andrii Danylenko

For more information on this series, please visit:
academicstudiespress.com/ukrainian-studies

ACADEMIC
STUDIES
PRESS

NEW YORK ELEGIES

Ukrainian Poems on the City

Edited and with an introduction by
OSTAP KIN

Boston
2019

Library of Congress Cataloging-in-Publication Data

Names: Kin, Ostap, editor, writer of introduction.

Title: New York elegies : Ukrainian poems on the city / edited and with an introduction by Ostap Kin.

Description: Boston : Academic Studies Press, 2018. | Series: Ukrainian studies | Includes bibliographical references. | English and Ukrainian.

Identifiers: LCCN 2018035496 (print) | LCCN 2018048069 (ebook) | ISBN 9781618115959 (ebook) | ISBN 9781618115942 (hardcover) | ISBN 9781618118912 (paperback)

Subjects: LCSH: Ukrainian poetry—20th century—Translations into English. | Ukrainian poetry—20th century. | Ukrainian poetry—21st century—Translations into English. | Ukrainian poetry—21st century. | New York (N.Y.)—Poetry.

Classification: LCC PG3986.E3 (ebook) | LCC PG3986.E3 N49 2018 (print) | DDC 891.7/91308—dc23

LC record available at https://lccn.loc.gov/2018035496

On the cover: Arcadia Olenska-Petryshyn, "Dwellings I" (1958). The Ukrainian Museum, New York.

Cover design by Ivan Grave.

Book design by Kryon Publishing Services Pvt. Ltd.
http://www.kryonpublishing.com

Published by Academic Studies Press in 2019.
28 Montfern Avenue
Brighton, MA 02135, USA
press@academicstudiespress.com
www.academicstudiespress.com

This publication was made possible in part by the financial support of the Shevchenko Scientific Society, USA from the John and Elisabeth Chlopecky Fund.

For Polina

Acknowledgments

I would like to thank Vitaly Chernetsky for including this volume in the Ukrainian Studies series (and for his feedback on my manuscript), and Igor Nemirovsky, the Director of the Academic Studies Press, for agreeing to publish it. My gratitude extends to the ASP editors I was lucky to work with at different phases of the project: acquisition editors Oleh Kotsyuba, David Michelson, Faith Wilson Stein, and Ekaterina Yanduganova, copy editor Kathleen Heil, and production editor Kira Nemirovsky.

I want to thank Yasha Klots whose invitation to participate in a round-table on the representation of New York in literatures led me to editing this anthology. Thanks also to Olga Bertelsen, Serhiy Bilenky, Oleksandr Boron, Cole Fishman, Oleh Ilnytzkyj, Anya Karagulina, and Marko Turchyn for their help as I worked on the book.

This book would not be possible without the generous financial support of the Shevchenko Scientific Society of New York—I am grateful to the Publications Committee for their decision to subsidize this project.

Thanks to the artists Kateryna Krychevska-Rosandich, Zenowij Onyshkewych, Mikhail Turovsky, Anton Varga, and to the artists' heirs Mary Burliuk Holt, Walter Petryshyn, Ihor Radysh for permitting me to use the art included in this anthology. The New-York Historical Society provided and permitted me to use a photograph of Abram Manevich's work. New York's Shapiro Auctions provided the photograph of Mikhail Turovsky's artwork. Thanks to Olena Martynyuk, Maria Rewakowicz, and Maria Shust at the Ukrainian Museum in New York for helping obtain permissions and photographs of artworks, and to Oksana Pidsukha at the Museum of the Ukrainian Diaspora in Kyiv for providing the photograph of Krychevska-Rosandich's art piece.

I am grateful, too, for poets and translators: the former created these unique versions of the city in their poetry and the latter tackled the difficult task to re-construct, re-present, and re-write these images in a new way, in a different language. I am thankful to the poets and the poets' heirs for permitting me to use their work.

Every effort has been made to contact all copyright holders. Any errors or omissions brought to my attention will be amended in future editions.

I would be remiss if this acknowledgement did not pay a special tribute to the very city of New York—for being an incessant harbor and powerful inspiration for the many creating in and outside the city.

Lastly, I would like to thank Polina Barskova for countless hours of flânerie and for our discussions of poets' turbulent worlds.

Ostap Kin

Table of Contents

Note on Transliteration

I use the conventional transliteration for names and locations in the body of the text. However, in the footnotes to my introduction, notes, and bibliographic information, I adhere to the Library of Congress system of transliteration.

In the introduction and notes, all translations are my own unless otherwise indicated.

Introduction: Mapping the Ukrainian Poetry of New York

In the midst of ever-increasing quantity, anthologies enable individual voices to be heard above the collective noise.
—Czeslaw Milosz[1]

In the very city of New York literally every day poets read their work in dozens of different places: at museums, churches, universities, various institutions, libraries, theatres, galleries, cafes and private places. [. . .] Every place that has a roof is a place for poetry.
—Bohdan Boychuk[2]

This poetry is no hymn to the homeland; rather the gaze of the allegorist, as it falls on the city, is the gaze of alienated man. It is the gaze of the flaneur, whose way of life still conceals behind a mitigating nimbus the coming desolation of the big-city dweller.
—Walter Benjamin[3]

The Encounter

Legend has it that on a mid-fall day in 1966, while on an official trip to New York City as part of the Soviet-Ukrainian delegation to the annual convention of the United Nations, Ivan Drach—then a thirty-year-old aspiring poet and screenwriter—managed to escape the KGB personnel tailing the poet and headed into a district of the city totally unknown to him. After wandering around this strange neighborhood, the poet stopped before a cafeteria, entered it, and spotted a bearded, bespectacled man sitting in the corner as if waiting for someone. Drach approached him; the two men shook hands. The bearded man, believed to be the American poet Allen Ginsberg, lived nearby in an area known as the East Village. The Ukrainian poet did not know conversational English well, and Ginsberg did not know any Ukrainian. So the two sat for an hour in complete silence, just gazing at each other, and afterwards stood up and bid their farewell, noiselessly parting ways.

---

1   Czeslaw Milosz, *Milosz's ABC*, trans. Madeline G. Levine (New York: Farrar, Straus and Giroux, 2001), 39.
2   Bohdan Boychuk, "Tsikavyi lyst," *Suchasnist'* 6 (1979): 102.
3   Walter Benjamin, The Arcades Project, trans. Howard Eiland and Kevin McLaughlin (Cambridge and London: Harvard University Press, 2002), 10.

The legend is incredible enough to have actually taken place. (What happened for sure, though, is that Drach did read at the international literary festival in Sorrento, Italy, in July 1967, along with Allen Ginsberg and the Austrian poet Ingeborg Bachmann. Later, the whole group of poets set out to meet the great American literary expatriate, Ezra Pound.[4]) How could these two important poets of their generation—one American, one Ukrainian—relate to each other? How was their silent yet meaningful encounter influenced by their environment—a cafeteria in Manhattan, a locale designated for such chance encounters, these meetings and almost-meetings? The appeal of this anecdote—not unlike perhaps the most important urban poem of the modern age, "À une Passante" ("To a Passerby") by Charles Baudelaire—lies in its desire to find the ideal urban language.

This anthology is dedicated to such encounters between the poets and the city.

The anthology's title is inspired by two poems contained in the collection, which bear two vital thematic components: the city of New York and the genre of elegy. An elegy is a poem about distance (and, in its original meaning, about death and mourning). In his volume *A Poet's Glossary*, Edward Hirsch defines the elegy as "a poem of mortal loss and consolation" and suggests that "[t]he American elegist in particular seems to suffer from [...] a 'polar privacy,' a dark sense of isolation, of displacement from traditional settings of grief and the consolations of community."[5] It may be risky but worth trying to amend Hirsch's definition to substitute American elegists for Ukrainian elegists in America or simply for Ukrainian elegists, too. It helps us understand that periods of drastic life changes—such as immigration, escape, and exile—will have a serious impact on the author from which a new sense of lyrical optics emerges. I want to call this new sense an elegy.[6] Ukrainian poets kept in mind that the elegy is defined by distance. For these poets, the city of New York had never really been *their* city but that did not deter them. Their writing, in the end, suggests a loving elegy for a city (an urban object

---

4   Interview with Ivan Drach in Koncha-Ozerna, July 2017.
5   Edward Hirsch, *A Poet's Glossary* (Boston: Houghton Mifflin Harcourt, 2014), 196, 198.
6   It has been also suggested that "New York poems might be by nature elegiac, at least for the writing of native New Yorkers, in that so many of the places in them were the haunts of—and then became haunted by—the poet's childhood" (John Hollander, "Foreword," in *I Speak of the City: Poems of New York*, Stephen Wolf, ed. [New York: Columbia University Press, 2007], xxv).

of desire) that they cannot fully appropriate. This distance, or even lack, only sharpens their appreciation.

The Roots of Ukrainian Poetry about New York

Ukrainian poetry written about and in New York developed more or less in parallel with the establishment of the Ukrainian community in the city. It might even be ventured that as soon as a community settles in an area, it works to establish some sort of printing press. Different diasporic waves produced different kinds of publications. With the first wave of Ukrainian immigration, which took place at the end of the nineteenth century predominantly from what is now known as Western Ukraine, came one of the first Ukrainian newspapers to be published on the East Coast; the New York-based *Svoboda* was established in 1893 and continues to be in print. The first wave of immigration had little cultural output but nonetheless managed to establish points that would later be transformed into a net of Ukrainian institutions in the city.[7] In addition, the twentieth century brought the poetic voice to the forefront of the Ukrainian diaspora. With each new wave and generation, Ukrainian diasporic poetry gained complexity, volume, and significance, culminating after World War II, with the appearance of the Third Wave.

New York City is powerfully associated with culture and literature at large, and poetry in particular. The city hosts a variety of *places of poetry* (such as publishing houses, reading venues, libraries, and even book clubs).[8] Newcomers to the city, belonging to differing backgrounds, interacted with the city's cultural aura to create both immigrant communities and literature about their experiences. Ukrainian literature in and about New York was no exception: it made its mark with the creation of journals, publishing houses, readings series, and, most importantly, ardent discussion, through which the city's writers were able to encounter their audiences.

---

7   On the account of the development of Ukrainian literature in the United States, see George Grabowicz, "The Voices of Ukrainian Émigré Poetry," *Canadian Slavonic Papers* 28, no. 2 (June 1986): 157–173; George S. N. Luckyj, *Ukrainian Literature in the Twentieth Century: A Reader's Guide* (Toronto: Shevchenko Scientific Society; University of Toronto Press, 1992), esp. chap. 7, "The Second Emigration and Diaspora," 95–103; Bohdan Rubchak, "Literatura." *Entsyklopediia Ukrains'koi diaspory*, Vol. 1, *Spolucheni Shtaty Ameryky, A–K*, 39–46 (New York: Naukove Tovarystvo im. Shevchenka v Amerytsi, 2009).

8   For a useful attempt of history and periodization of literature written in New York City, see Susan Edmiston and Linda D. Cirino, *Literary New York: A History and Guide* (Layton, UT: Gibbs Smith Publishers, 1991).

So how was the city portrayed by these poets? What lenses did they use for their observations and expressions?[9] Those who came to stay and those who came to visit approached cities in different ways. Historically, the Ukrainian diaspora in the twentieth century gravitated around three major hubs—Warsaw, Prague, and New York—and a few less significant but nonetheless important cities such as Berlin, London, and Paris.[10] New York served as a crucial harbor for Ukrainians from the end of the nineteenth century to the present day—both for those who decided to immigrate and those who wanted to travel and encounter the "New World." Literati of various inclinations, poets included, were among those displaced. And each poet had a different story, a separate and intimate encounter with the city.

Outlining the Goals

New York Elegies: Ukrainian Poetry on the City, an anthology of Ukrainian poetry about New York City, includes poems written by Ukrainian poets between 1922 and 2016.[11] The anthology presents an almost century-long

---

9   For a source of scholarly discussions of various themes in regard to the city of New York, see Cyrus R. K. Patell and Bryan Waterman, eds. *The Cambridge Companion to Literature of New York* (Cambridge, UK: Cambridge University Press, 2010).

10   The cities of political, cultural, and other dominance outside of Ukraine are a topic yet to be researched. Here, we can only outline the possibilities suggested by scholars of the Ukrainian community in exile. George Luckyj lists the following North American cities: New York, Philadelphia, Chicago, Detroit, Montreal, Toronto, and Winnipeg (George Luckyj, *Ukrainian Literature in Twentieth Century: A Reader's Guide* [Toronto: University of Toronto Press, 1992]); Maria Rewakowicz suggests another triangle of cities significant to the Ukrainian diaspora: New York, Warsaw, and Prague (Maria Rewakowicz, *Literature, Exile, Alterity: The New York Group of Poets* [Boston: Academic Studies Press, 2014]).

11   A list of selected anthologies of American poetry about New York City may include (but does not limit itself to) the following publications: *The City That Never Sleeps: Poems of New York*, edited by Shawkat M. Toorawa, foreword by Anne Pierson Wiese (Albany: State University of New York Press, 2015); *Writing New York: A Literary Anthology*, edited by Philipp Lopate (New York: Library of America, 2008); *I Speak of the City: Poems of New York*, selected and edited by Stephen Wolf, foreword by John Hollander (New York: Columbia University Press, 2007); *Broken Lands: Poems of Brooklyn*, edited by Julia Spicher Kasdorf and Michael Tyrell, foreword by Hal Sirowitz (New York: New York University Press, 2007); *New York Poets II: An Anthology: From Edwin Denby to Bernadette Mayer*, edited by Mark and Trevor Winkfield (Manchester: Carcanet, 2006); *The New York Poets: Frank O'Hara, John Ashbery, Kenneth Koch, James Schuyler: An Anthology*, edited with an introduction by Mark Ford (Manchester: Carcanet, 2004); *Poetry After 9-11: An Anthology of New York Poets*, edited by Dennis Loy Johnson, introduction by Alicia Ostriker (New York: Melville House, 2002); *Poems of New York*, selected and edited by Elizabeth Schmidt (New York: Alfred A. Knopf, 2002);

corpus of poetic text, including works by poets belonging to three distinct waves of Ukrainian immigration to the United States, visiting poets from Soviet Ukraine, and poets who moved or traveled to the United States after the 1991 collapse of the Soviet Union, when Ukraine regained its independence.

New York Elegies aims to shed light on the previously unexamined space of Ukrainian literature by providing examples of poetic works in both the Ukrainian original and the English translation for scholars of Slavic literatures, urban studies, and diaspora studies, and for those with a interest in poetry. This anthology highlights how, despite and/or due to a number of historical and political obstacles, Ukrainian literature over the course of past century proved reactive to contemporary international literary tendencies. This collection of poems about the Ukrainian New York offers a multi-layered panorama of fresh urban visions, comprised of texts composed by poets who had (or continue to have) diverse fates. *New York Elegies* attempts to demonstrate how descriptions and evocations of New York City are connected to various stylistic modes and topical questions urgent to Ukrainian poetry throughout its development. The collection thus gives readers the opportunity to view New York through various poetic and stylistic lenses.[12]

The texts are grouped into three sections: (a) interwar poetry from the early 1920s through the late 1930s, written by visiting poets from Soviet Ukraine and émigré poets based in the United States, as well as by poets who never visited New York, such as Mykhail Semenko and Oleksa Slisarenko; (b) post-World War II poetry, written predominantly by newly emigrated poets from Ukraine who left during the war, as well as by visiting Soviet Ukrainian poets between the mid-1940s and mid-1970s; and (c) post-1991

New York: Poems, edited by Howard Moss (New York: Avon, 1980); *An Anthology of New York Poets*, edited by Ron Padgett and David Shapiro (New York: Random House, 1970). Of particular interest are early individual collections and anthologies dedicated to New York that date back to the late 1900s and 1920s, such as *Ballads of Old New York*, ed. Arthur Guiterman (New York: Harper & Bros., 1920); *City Tides*: Archie Austin Coates (New York: George H. Doran Company, 1918); *Cobblestones*: David Sentner (New York: Alfred A. Knopf, 1921); *Manhattan*, ed. John Myers O'Hara (Portland, ME: Smith & Sale, 1915); Charles Hanson Towne *Manhattan* (New York: M. Kennerley, 1909).

12 A useful approach might be a comparison between how American writers and those who arrived to New York viewed and depicted the city; see Stephen Miller, *Walking New York: Reflections of American Writers from Walt Whitman to Teju Cole* (New York: Fordham University Press, 2015).

poetry written by both visiting and immigrating poets from a newly independent Ukraine.

The poems belonging to the first period are characterized by their close connection to the Futurist tradition emerging at that time in Ukraine and cultivated among Ukrainian authors residing in the United States. For example, one of the most prolific Ukrainian New York-based poets of the time, Mykola Tarnovsky, described in detail his Leftist views on the city's turbulent nature. Tarnovsky was employed by Ukrainian leftist organizations and edited several magazines, some of which were dedicated to literature. In the texts by these left-leaning authors, the city serves as a place for the political and social to manifest itself. Futurist aesthetics and socialist politics become intertwined. Although these poets were enthralled with the city's flashing lights, they also opposed what they believe to be a sharp division between the city's rich and poor, the privileged and the outcast.

The second section contains a significant number of poets, both established and emerging, who fled Ukraine during World War II. The established poets include authors such as Yuri Kosach, Yevhen Malanyuk, and Vadym Lesych, to name a few. These poets published their first books during the interwar period of the 1920s and 1930s.[13] Their move west was crucial for their actual survival and, no less significant, for the survival of their creative oeuvre. Those who belong to the group of emerging poets (for example, the New York Group of poets, which I will turn to later) are those who left Ukraine as teenagers, received their education in the West, and thus had different perspective toward literature, Ukrainian or otherwise.

These two groups disagreed on several questions: Which direction should the poetic gaze look to in the situation of exile? And what is to be done with the constructed feeling of nostalgia? According to Svetlana Boym, nostalgia is "an affective yearning for a community with a collective memory, a longing for a continuity in a fragmented world. Nostalgia inevitably reappears as a defense mechanism in a time of accelerated rhythms of life and historical upheavals."[14] In other words, should Ukrainian diasporic poetry be nostalgic, fueled by the memories of the Past, yearning for the abandoned realm of Ukrainian territory and culture? Or should it be urgent, directed at the poet's new environment, that of

---

13 For a take on Iurii Kosach's life in the immigration and the writer's adaptation to a new world, see Askold Melnyczuk, "Remembering and Forgetting," *Boston Globe*, April 4, 2015. https://www.bostonglobe.com/arts/books/2015/04/04/remembering-and-forgetting/XqrhKryvRSCUxi7xqmWMLK/story.html (accessed: November 30, 2017).

14 Svetlana Boym, *The Future of Nostalgia* (New York: Basic Books), xiv.

New York urbanity? The older group of poets portrayed the city with the sentiments of those who had been made to leave their home—with loneliness, resentment, a lack of understanding, difficulty accepting their new situation, and a sense of being lost. In contrast, the younger generation felt more open toward new stylistic means and devices, delving into modern literary approaches to urban representation. Sometimes, their poems were free of any specific topographical details, yet were ostensibly based on their experience of making contact with New York (for example, Yuriy Tarnawsky, Bohdan Boychuk, Bohdan Rubchak, Dima, Lydia Palij, and others). It is important to mention here the New York Group of poets, a modernist circle of young authors. This group, united in their quest for new literary styles and sensitivities, opposed the representatives from older generations of the Ukrainian diaspora and their somewhat old-fashioned approach to the understanding of literature and its processes.[15] The poetry of the younger generations, however, offered a new and timely contribution to the development of Ukrainian poetry in the Diaspora.[16]

The following excerpts demonstrate how the youngest generation of poets of that time living in the Diaspora viewed the city:

> tearing apart her cotton dress
> she crosses Times Square
> and gives herself to everyone
> who hungers for flesh
> and pays
>
> you
> also make love to her
> having no one
> closer[17]

And this excerpt from Dima:

> The night is sliced, split into half

---

15 For a history and critical study of the body of work produced by the New York Group of poets, see Maria Rewakowicz, *Literature, Exile, Alterity*; and Mariia Revakovych [Maria Rewakowicz], *Persona Non-grata* (Kyiv: Krytyka, 2012).

16 To compare and get an understanding of the establishment of literary life in New York that apparently overlapped with the formation of literary life among Ukrainian immigrants of the post-World War II wave, see Dan Wakefield, *New York in the 50s* (Boston: Houghton Mifflin/Seymour Lawrence, 1992).

17 Bohdan Boychuk, "Eleven," trans. Mark Rudman and the author, p. 125 in this volume.

by the roar of engines, the wail of sirens,
by the mad traffic of
the New York cars
and the smoke from house
on fire close by.
The night ended
without ever dreaming.[18]

As well as one from Lydia Palij:

In the canyons of the city,
the brownstones
breathe fish and garlic
on each other.
On the asphalt

[...]

Wide-hipped black women
sit on the stoops
near open doors,
knees splayed apart.

[...]

Dark-skinned kiddos
screech under the cascades
from the open hydrants.[19]

All three poems focus on the dynamics of street movement. Palij's description concentrates on an unnamed area of the city where life goes on in the heat of the summer, with the block's residents filling the street. This image is both concrete, yet located in an unknown place; its precise location is not necessary for the reader to know. Boychuk looks at the city from the point of view of a prostitute who is a city dweller and a flaneuse, walking along Forty-Second Street in Manhattan. In the Dima poem, the body of the city is stripped of any human bodies and filled with invisible drivers whose cars cause "[...] the roar of engines, / the wail of sirens" as well as "[...] the mad traffic of." These poems present us with the city's shocking, sometime uneasy intimacy.

---

18 Dima, "New York Night," trans. Ostap Kin and Ali Kinsella, p. 135 in this volume.
19 Lida Palij, "A Hot Day in New York," trans. Ostap Kin and Ali Kinsella, p. 137 in this volume.

Poets visiting from Soviet Ukraine following World War II and during the Cold War, composed a vital and significant bulk of poetry on the city. By and large, these poets were expected to represent the official Soviet worldview and were commissioned to fulfill a particular (and often, ideological) undertaking (e.g. to promote and defend the ideals of a socialist world and to persuade the Ukrainian community of New York City that events in Soviet Ukraine were part of a historical process and that the issues of concern in the Ukrainian diaspora—like, for example, the process of violent Russification or imprisonment of dissidents— was not threatening).[20] Each poet had to make a near impossible decision: on the one hand, they likely wished to portray the city as authentically as possible, but, on the other hand, were supposed to meet the standards of Communist Party propaganda. They were expected, in other words, to uphold the correct— that is, Soviet—style of life and condemn what they experienced in New York. Sometimes these poems are curious in their ambivalent utterances, compromising and uniting the authentic with the ideological (as might be the case of Borys Oliynyk). Yuri (George) Shevelov had his own take on this specifically "Soviet" view of the American city. In an article written in response to the publication of several of Andriy Malyshko's poems (in the Polish, Paris-based literary journal, *Kultura*, in 1950), Shevelov accounts for Malyshko's poetry and sets himself up as a defender of New York City, which faithfully served as a home for him from the early 1950s until his demise in 2002. Shevelov writes:

> This America arrived into the Malyshko book not from the New York streets, but from the pages of the Moscow-based journal *Krokodil* [*Crocodile*]. It is not interesting for us. We know it. Mayakovsky created it during the first years following the revolution with his colleagues at the office of ROSTA [*Russian telegraph agency*]. Back then such an embodiment was known under the name of Wilson. Mayakovsky predicted the world's future as struggle between a Russian Ivan and an American Wilson, a struggle in which the victor Ivan raises Soviet flag above Chicago. No one believes in such an America. [...] This image is a central one in Soviet propaganda and appears in many volumes of literature even when a cylinder and binoculars are not actually mentioned.[21]

---

20 For an example of a volume comprised of works depicting the United States and New York, specifically, in an unbalanced light, see *Gorod Zheltogo D'iavola: Sovetskie literatory ob amerikanskom obraze zhizni*, Anatolii Parpara, ed. (Moscow: Khudozhestvennaia literatura, 1984).

21 Iurii Shevelov, "Zakhid ie Zakhid, a Skhid ie Skhid," in Iurii Shevelov, *Literaturoznavstvo:*

A group of Soviet Ukrainian poets including Andriy Malyshko, Ivan Drach, Dmytro Pavlychko, and Borys Oliynyk wrote poems about the city after their New York sojourns, which spanned the mid-1940s through the 1980s.[22] Their trips often resulted in single poems or cycles, but also full-length poetry collections, as in the cases of Andriy Malyshko and Ivan Drach.[23] Regardless of the heavily-politicized verse published, these poets crafted nuanced, differing depictions of the Other from a Soviet angle.

The third section of poems belongs to the period after the collapse of the Soviet Union. The post-1991 period is characterized by the newly available—and until then, unimaginable—opportunities that opened up for poets, who became free to travel around the world. Thus, the poems in this section are divided among those who, due to various circumstances, decided to settle down in New York or elsewhere in the United States (for example, Vasyl Makhno and Oksana Lutshyshyna), and those visiting poets who belonged to at least three generations of the Ukrainian diaspora: *visimdesiatnyky*, or the Eighties generation (Yuri Andrukhovych and Oksana Zabuzhko), *dev'iatdesiatnyky*, or the Nineties generation (Serhiy Zhadan, Maryana Savka, and others), and *dvokhtysiachnyky*, or the millennium generation (Kateryna Babkina, Iryna Shuvalova, Iryna Vikyrchak).

This post-1991 poetry is characterized by the poets' experiences in a new, turbulent, and unpredictable post-Soviet world. These poets were, by and large, free of the burdens that impacted generations of Soviet Ukrainian poets; many of these émigré poets were unable to return to Ukraine and thus their writings often focused on an irresolvable sense of nostalgia, longing for the old country and its traditions, and searching for a new home. In the new era of the 1990s (and even now, in the first two decades of the twenty-first century), Ukrainian poets no longer have to fear eternal displacement or be scared of forced residency in a new and often hostile environment. They observe New York not with fear but with an acute feeling of curiosity and even awe as they search for new aesthetics to reflect their discoveries. In this hyperactive epoch

---

knyha II, compiled by Ivan Dziuba (Kyiv: Vydavnychyi dim "Kyievo-Mohylians'ka akademiia," 2009), 520–521.

22 In general, the topic of encounter of Soviet and émigré literati as well as the relationship between those two groups of literary people needs an attentive study. It suffices to say that every such trip of Soviet authors to the United States have been covered in the Ukrainian media in the United States and led to ongoing disputes.

23 Andrii Malyshko, *Za synim morem* (Kyiv: Radians'kyi pys'mennyk, 1950); Ivan Drach, *Amerykans'kyi zoshyt* (Kyiv: Molod', 1979).

of technology, Tony Judt suggests that New York is the city that "looks outward, and thus attractive to people who would not feel comfortable further inland."[24]

Mapping Ukrainian New York

Historically, New York City has functioned as a harbor—both physically and symbolically—for newcomers. It has played this role for centuries with immigrants coming in on vast ships at first, and now on aircrafts. By and large, the city continues to perform its role as a harbor; if one likes it here, they remain, and if not, they continue further inland. Even if New York was not the traveler's initial destination, the memory of the city remained as their first impression of the United States.

The city—and, more specifically, certain neighborhoods—remains one of the most ethnically diverse urban areas in the world. Jackson Heights in Queens has proudly held this title for decades. Specific neighborhoods throughout the city's five boroughs are home to dynamic and diverse diasporic groups. East Harlem and Bushwick in Brooklyn are associated with Latino immigrants, while Yorkshire on the Upper East Side used to be an enclave for German migrants. Italians established what became known as "Little Italy" both in Manhattan and later in Brooklyn's Bay Ridge district (though Bay Ridge is now home to an Arabic population from various regions of the world). Greenpoint in Brooklyn and Ridgewood in Queens have become home to the Polish diaspora. Brighton Beach and Sheepshead Bay in southern Brooklyn are notoriously marked as areas of influence for people from the former Soviet Union. Chinatown in Manhattan, Chinatown in Brooklyn's Sunset Park, and Flushing in Queens should be mentioned too, as well as Korean Way (or, as it is officially known, West 32nd Street) in Manhattan; East Williamsburg, Bushwick, Borough's Park, and Riverdale in the Bronx are the city's well-known Hasidic enclaves. Finally, the East Village in Manhattan and, more recently, Staten Island, house much of the Ukrainian diaspora.

Ukrainians are commonly believed to have arrived in the United States for the first time in the 1880 to 1890s. These immigrants were largely from Galicia, then part of Austria-Hungary and now part of Western Ukraine. Although most of these newcomers from what is now Ukraine were working class, they nonetheless created the foundation for cultural and educational life for future

---

24 Tony Judt, *The Memory Chalet* (London: William Heinemann, 2010), 196.

generations.[25] By the end of nineteenth century there were newspapers, various organizations, and churches on both coasts of the United States. Revolution in the Russian Empire impacted the United States as well, for many of these immigrants were manual laborers seeking a more comfortable life; the idealization and adherence to first socialist and later communist ideals was popular.

In the years following the end of World War II, Ukrainians started to gradually move to New York and established or continued to establish a thriving Ukrainian community in Manhattan's East Village. For decades, this neighborhood has been closely affiliated with Eastern European immigrants and particularly with Ukrainian emigres. Residents of the East Village experienced a wide range of cultural features characteristic for the Ukrainian community from the 1960s through the 1990s. You could visit dive bars and affordable restaurants with Eastern European cuisine. You could acquire art by Ukrainian artists from the gallery and shop ARKA. You could buy various editions of books in the bookstore Surma.[26] You could even purchase a trip to Soviet Ukraine through the Kovbasiuk travel agency, or attend exhibitions by Ukrainian artists, or listen to poetry readings or literary discussions at The Literary and Arts Club on Second Avenue in those days, just as can now be done at the Ukrainian Museum or the Ukrainian Institute of America.[27]

Scholarly institutions that previously existed in Ukraine were reestablished in New York, such as the Shevchenko Scientific Society, now located in the East Village, and the Ukrainian Academy of Arts and Science on the Upper West Side, while some were created from scratch, such as the Ukrainian Institute of America. In the 1950s, the Organization of Ukrainian Writers in Exile "Slovo," was established as well. A great number of newspapers, literary

25 For the history of Ukrainian immigration to the United States, see Iulian Bachyns'kyi, *Ukrains'ka immihratsiia v Spoluchenkh Shtatkh Ameryky* (Kyiv, 1995); Myron Kuropas, *The Ukrainian Americans: Roots and Aspirations, 1884–1954* (Toronto: University of Toronto Press, 1991); Halyna Lemekh, *Ukrainian Immigrants in New York: Collision of Two Worlds* (El Paso, TX: LFB Scholarly Publishing, 2010).
26 One of the oldest and last remaining venues from the great Ukrainian past in New York was a bookstore called Surma. Located in the East Village, it closed in 2016. For coverage of the event, see Noah Remnick, "With Closing of East Village Shop, Little Ukraine Grows Smaller," *New York Times*, June 5, 2016. Available online: https://www.nytimes.com/2016/06/06/nyregion/with-closing-of-east-village-shop-little-ukraine-grows-smaller.html?mcubz=0 (accessed on November 30, 2017). See also an older article on the Surma bookstore: Alastair Reid, "An Afternoon in the Ukraine," *New Yorker*, May 31, 1982, 27.
27 Christine Lukomsky, "The Ukrainian East Village: Present," *Нові горизонти*/New Directions 3, no. 7 (1971): 11–23.

journals, and scholarly publications were produced with the help of this second wave of Ukrainian émigrés.

These publications confronted the long-standing Ukrainian New York-based leftist presses and organizations. Leon Tolopko started off as a poet, and after World War I, involved himself in Ukrainian socialist institutions based in New York. Tolopko went on to edit a newspaper and publish several volumes of history on the Ukrainian leftist movement in the United States.[28] At the end of the 1950s, Mykola Tarnovsky traveled to Soviet Ukraine and remained there until his death, enjoying relative literary success: his works were reprinted in many collections and translated into the other languages of the Soviet Union.[29]

Mykola Tarnovsky decided to visit and then remain in the Soviet Ukraine. Yuri Kosach, nephew to the famous Ukrainian writer Lesia Ukrainka, traveled to Soviet Ukraine on several occasions in the 1960s. His works were even published in Soviet Ukraine, from the 1960s through the1980s, making him an anomaly—typically, Ukrainian diasporic writers were not received well by Soviet critics. Kosach could have remained in Soviet Ukraine to enjoy the success and attention of the Soviet Union, as Tarkovsky did. He did not need to struggle in his adopted country, the United States, but nevertheless always returned—proving that he chose freedom.

Common Places/Common Senses

We certainly can speak of the "Kyiv text" or the "Kharkiv text" or the "Lviv text"[30]—for centuries, these were the important hubs for Ukrainian (and other

---

28 For the history of Ukrainian socialist and communist movement in the United States, see Leon Tolopko, *Trudovi ukraintsi SShA: Knyha persha (1980–1924 rr.)* (New York: Liha amerykans'kykh ukraintsiv, 1984) and its English-language version: Leon Tolopko, *Working Ukrainians in the USA: book I (1980–1924)* (New York: Ukrainian American League, 1986).

29 See, for example, Tarnovsky's "Avtobiohrafiia" (Autobiography) in a volume of his selected works: Mykola Tarnovs'kyi, *Z burkhlyvykh liv* (Kyiv: Dnipro, 1965).

30 For the Kyiv text, see Taras Koznarsky, "Three Novels, Three Cities." In Irena R. Makaryk and Virlana Tkacz, eds. *Modernism in Kyiv: Jubilant Experimentation* (Toronto: University of Toronto Press, 2010), 98–137. Inna Bulkina 'Kievskii tekst v russkom romantizme: Problemy tipologii,' *Lotmanovskii sbornik* 3 (Moscow: OGI, 2004), 93–104. Serhiy Bilenky, *Imperial Urbanism in the Borderlands: Kyiv, 1800–1905* (Toronto: University of Toronto Press, 2018); for the Lviv text, see Jan Paul Hinrichs, *Lemberg—Lwów—Lviv* ([Amsterdam]: Lubberhuizen, 2008), and its Ukrainian edition: Ian-Paul' Hinrikhs [Jan Paul Hinrikhs], *Lemberg — Lwów — Lviv. Fatal'ne misto,* trans. Iaroslav Dovhopolyi (Kyiv:

kinds of) literature and poetry—but what about the cities outside of and away from Ukraine? Many Ukrainian authors flowed from its territories westward (and sometimes eastward), establishing literary hubs in foreign countries. New York is an example of the results of this flow.

What is a city's text? Vladimir N. Toporov provides a useful definition: "It [here Toporov specifically means St. Petersburg, but this can also be applied to New York] talks to us through [or with] its streets, squares, waters, islands, gardens, buildings, monuments, people, history, ideas and can be understood as in its sense a heterogeneous text which is ascribed a certain general meaning and on a basis of which one could reconstruct a certain system of signs that is realized in a text."[31]

When paging through the anthology, one notices which urban patterns catch the attention of many generations of Ukrainian poets; these are topics and rubrics that, despite various literary styles and political affiliations, nonetheless linked many of the Ukrainian poets in New York together, comprising an echo chamber that we might name the "Ukrainian poetic text of New York."

Topics "traveling" from decade to decade include: (a) modern features of the city, such as the subway, lack of nature, skyscrapers, bridges, lighting, and advertisements; (b) addressing the great writers of New York, and borrowing from their arsenal of writing, for example Edgar Allan Poe, Walt Whitman, Federico Garcia Lorca, and Vladimir Mayakovsky, among others; (c) features of ethnic and racial difference like Harlem, blackness, poverty, social inequality, and injustice; (d) toponyms: Broadway, Brooklyn, Central Park, Hudson River, East River, Times Square, and Wall Street (a location especially significant to the poetry of left-leaning poets, who believed it to be the manifestation of capitalism, a place from which exploitation emanates); and (e) various natural and human-made features surrounding and defining the city, such as the harbor, ocean, and islands.

It is curious to note that many of these topics occur in both Ukrainian and American literatures on New York. Some of the overlapping topics discussed include "the city's contradictory faces of glamour and squalor," "the gigantic

---

Vydavnytstvo Oleksiia Zhupans'koho, 2010); Katarzyna Kotyńska, *Lwów. O odczytywaniu miasta na nowo* (Kraków: Międzynarodowe Centrum Kultury, 2015) and its Ukrainian translation: Katazhyna Kotyns'ka [Katarzyna Kotyńska], *L'viv: perechytuvannia mista*, trans. Ostap Slyvyns'kyi (L'viv: Vydavnytstvo Staroho Leva, 2017).

31 Vladimir Toporov, "Peterburg i Peterburgskii tekst russkoi literatury." In *Mif. Ritual. Simvol. Obraz* (Moscow: Izdatel'skaia gruppa "Progress"—"Kul'tura"), 274– 275.

built environment and the relative unimportance of nature," "its Mammon-like preoccupation with business and money," "its offer of anonymity to the many," "its large, dense population, providing space if not always the warmest of welcomes for the immigrant and the nonconformist," "its fabled loneliness and alienation," and "its symbolic importance as the modernist city par excellence."[32]

For the purposes of this anthology, the city is, first and foremost, a zone of imagination and only secondly a place of experience. A symptom of this is the inclusion of poems by those who never visited New York. For them, the city was a powerful chimera, a product of a cultural imagination that they needed to re-imagine. Onto this symbolic canvas, they projected their fears, dreams, and anxieties of the ideal modernist urban body. Poetry written by those who never visited the city is one of the more curious subcategories included in this anthology—those who instead imagined it, creating by means of fantasy. It is crucial to keep in mind that relationship with the urban image and urban dynamics were at the very center of the concerns of the Ukrainian poetic futurism; one can argue, even, that the urban attraction here was even more powerful and productive than with the Russian futurists. For Ukrainian poets, the modern city was both necessary and unattainable—hence, this constant attraction, and it is within this context that New York became the ultimate modern dream.

Imagining New York from afar was in literary fashion in the 1920s. Franz Kafka established the fashion's precedent a decade prior with his text *Amerika*, which he wrote without ever visiting. In Ukraine, New York grabbed the attention of poets as well as prose writers. Mykhail Semenko, for one, did not need to visit the city for it to leave vivid traces in his poetic oeuvre. His radical visual poetry outspokenly demonstrates and maps the city of New York as crucial to futurist poetry. Another example is a poem by Oleksa Slisarenko, who also never visited New York.[33] He observes the city through the poetry of Walt Whitman, who also influenced a number of Ukrainian poets in the twentieth century. Slisarenko's poem, first published in 1923, suggests, at first glance, the strong literary impact of Whitman on Ukrainian literature.

---

32 Philip Lopate, "Introduction," in Philip Lopate, ed., *Writing New York: A Literary Anthology* (New York: Library of America, 1998), xviii-xix.

33 For the contribution to the Ukrainian branch of futurism by Mykhail' Semenko and Oleksa Slisarenko, see Oleh S. Ilnytzkyj, *Ukrainian Futurism, 1914–1930* (Cambridge, MA: Harvard Ukrainian Research Institute, 1997).

The City's Boundaries and the Echoing of
September 11, 2001 Tragedy

At times, imagining and imaging New York becomes akin to imagining the end of the world, the city seemed that remote and that terrific, almost impossible. For poets, the imaginary New York connects the real and surreal, utopian and dystopian impulses, dreams and anxieties. It is that utopian "good place" (*eu topos*), that end/edge of the world that never ceases to attract people all over:

> Have driven
> across the bridge
> effortlessly,
> without having to pay
> the toll,
> like blood
> coming
> out of vein,
> the car
> tumbles along
> the concrete
> as if through space,
> other cars, trucks
> tumble past me,
> some hundred
> yards ahead
> where the darkness
> starts
> a sign
> in red, blue, and white
> on a green
> background
> proclaims:
> INTERSTATE
> 80 WEST
> RT 17 NEWARK
> EXIT
> 1/2 MILE.[34]

34   Yuriy Tarnawsky, "End of the World," trans. by the author, p. 103 in this volume.

By constructing the end/edge as both spatial and temporal, New York is imaged here as an end in itself — that is, the reality beyond this megapolis is literally beyond imagination. We may also encounter risqué play with the dystopian New York in a poem by Yuri Andrukhovych, one of the city's most observant Ukrainian describers. He imagines the city being destroyed by the lyrical character:

"It's New York" — I say. —
"Prepare for bombing."

We start, not at the same time,
but all four of us. The streams cross,
the city beneath us hisses and whole neighborhoods

go out.
"More attention to Manhattan" — I say. —
"Black Harlem and the Bronx are not to be touched."
"Brooklyn and Queens are down" —
adds John,

a bit drunker and more concentrated.
Having demolished Chrysler, Seagram and the Empire State,
we are generally satisfied with the operation.
We pull up our zips, we go back
to base, in darkness, feeling like the aces of creation.[35]

Something that was meant as a simple joke in the end turns into horrifying tragedy: "One month later— / such jokes are in bad taste." Andrukhovych's poem rehearses the point made by one of the city's cultures main theoreticians: his work's imagining of the destruction of New York can now be seen as a macabre foreshadowing of the terror attacks of 9/11. Once the Western nightmare of the twentieth century became a reality—with Manhattan destroyed—the city needed to be reimagined altogether. "Many portrayals of the city's end are born of love for the city, not disgust." […] "[I]n the summer months [of 2001], American image makers portrayed disasters that were remarkably similar to what was to happen in September. Up to the very moment of the attacks on 9/11, these fantasies seemed irresistible to writers and filmmakers."[36]

---

35   Yuri Andrukhovych, "Bombing New York City," trans. Sarah Luczaj, p. 181 in this volume.
36   Max Page, *The City's End: Two Centuries of Fantasies, Fears, and Premonitions of New York's Destruction* (New Haven, CT: Yale University Press, 2008) 146, 195.

The tragedy of 9/11 inspired mourning in American and non-American poets alike. In the United States, an anthology of poems about the city after 9/11 has been published. The city's greatest tragedy was not ignored by Ukrainian poets and writers, either; works by Yuri Andrukhovych, Vasyl Makhno, and Oksana Zabuzhko contain deliberations and personal emotional responses to 9/11. *New York Elegies* includes a poem by Yuri Andrukhovych, whose main New York elegiac theme circles closely around this topic. This poem is paired with a text by Vasyl Makhno, which might be thought of as a poetic response to Yuri Andrukhovych's verse.[37] Zabuzhko also tackles the topic in an elegy to freedom and strangeness, managing to capture a strikingly powerful image of the Towers as something that was "erected to be hit like bowling." Andrukhovych, too, wrote of Manhattan's loss of the Twin Towers: "The expansion of Manhattan in all its denseness and beauty now, after the fall of the Twins, cannot be seen. For me, in particular, this view is lost forever. I did not make it on time. When the Twins stood, I didn't come up with an idea to suffocate with them."[38]

For a number of foreign-born writers and poets from various corners of the globe, the events of 9/11 made them reconsider their place in the city. It made them feel like a New Yorker in the same way that President Kennedy proclaimed himself a Berliner when the German city was in danger.[39] Lithuanian poet and scholar Tomas Venclova felt this; for him, 9/11 let him explore a hitherto unknown side of his identity: "[o]n that day [September 11, 2001] I felt myself an American for the first time—there was a sentiment (*oshchushchenie*) that my country was under attack."[40]

In addition to the imaginary eschatological New York, there also exists the abstract poetic New York. How can one depict the city without mentioning its toponyms? This problem was outlined, in part, in the works of 1920s Soviet Ukrainian poets who never visited the city. The mechanism of this poetry is based on a wide array of literature, primarily poetic, the authors of which were usually American, such as Walt Whitman. The other prominent body of work is the poetry of the New York Group. Its members, according to the scholar Olena Haleta, "often point at specific places that are connected [to the history of the

---

37 See: "Aviation Response to Yuri Andrukhovych," in Vasyl Makhno, *Thread and Selected New York Poems*, trans. Orest Popovych (New York: Meeting Eyes Bindery, 2009).

38 Iurii Andrukhovych, *Leksykon intymnykh mist* (Kyiv: Meridian Czernowitz, 2011), 196–197.

39 Norman Manea, *The Fifth Impossibility* (New Haven, CT: Yale University Press), 320.

40 "[Interview with] Tomas Venclova." In *Poety v N'iu-Iorke: o gorode, iazyke, diaspore*, Iakov Klots, ed. (Moscow: Novoe literaturnoe obozrenie, 2016), 658.

group]. Their city's topography is above all the topography of Ukrainian New York, constructed by predecessors, contemporaries, and by the power of their own imagination."[41] One of the key figures in the group was Bohdan Rubchak. He knew the city and its topography well, but preferred to portray it abstractly as a symbol, rather than an object on a map. Rubchak came to the city as a teenager in the late 1940s and lived in Harlem, and worked as a professor of literature. The poetical lens of his poetry is modernist but stripped of physical presence, preferring a metaphysical one. His contribution to the anthology, "The Homeless," was published in his debut 1956 collection when the poet was just twenty-one. This work displays some of the most vivid urban verse of the poet's corpus. In the poem, Rubchak does not specify what city he is writing about—but is that kind of precision necessary for his vision? There are, however, a few indications that the city's environs are those of New York. The city's renowned movement and speed is mentioned ("[i]n his eyes there is a street that will never slow him down"); in popular media, New York is often depicted as the city that never sleeps. The poet reiterates this imagery in the fourth stanza: "This motley street will slow down for nothing." Here, Rubchak's use of the adjective "motley" adds a colorfulness to the depiction of the street's landscape.

A Soviet Look on New York as Text

I tend to believe that Soviet poets—those part of delegations and those who visited the city between the wars—were impressed and moved by the city. A 1967 poem by Pavlychko serves as a telling example. His writing is based on his first visit to the city in 1966; here, we are dealing with his freshest impressions of the city. The poet chose to work with the first philosophical element—air. On this canvas, the poet unrolls a brief story of a day in the life of the city. First, the origin of the air: "New York's air consists of clumps: / a canvas of smoke above the dumps." Here, the topic of nature reoccurs. Then, a Soviet look at the city: 'I was born and grew up in a large ancient city, but I like small American towns; the largest conglomerate of such a town is New York." And later, the poet elaborates: "New York is a thing in itself, a small settlement that grew large, an all-American open throughway (*prokhidnyi dvir*) with its own laws and its own inner life; but even for a sporadic visitor, New York is a spec-

---

41   Olena Haleta, *Vid antolohii do ontolohii: antolohiia iak sposib reprezentatsii ukrains'koi litera-tury kintsia XIX–pochatku XXI stolittia* (Kyiv: Smoloskyp, 2015), 274.

tacle, it is a theater for everyone where spectators and actors are divided very conditionally and all the time are changing roles."[42]

This anthology allows us to observe various motifs or topoi over time—for example, how Ukrainian immigrants and visitors of New York reacted to the phenomenon of Harlem, a locale of expressed racial difference in the city. For many reasons (some more obvious than others), Ukrainian poets in New York were fascinated by Harlem and its complex ethnic, social, political, aesthetic, and even sexual dynamics. Ukrainians, as newcomers and foreigners to the city, found this zone of otherness a useful comparison vis-à-vis their new place of habitation. The interpretations of Harlem in 1920s poetry are filled with conflicting expressions of adoration, anxiety, and attraction. Some poets lived there, others just visited; both parties, in the end, became well acquainted with the neighborhood. In this anthology, one can observe certain tendencies—both stylistic and thematic—as to how the borough was absorbed and digested in their writing.

In his poem "The Black Epic," Ivan Kulyk introduces a main character called Sambo, which is based on the children's book *The Story of Little Black Sambo* (1899). In this poem, Kulyk attempts to restore Sambo's path across the United States and tells Sambo's story of "how he cursed his fate of picking cotton on southern plantations, how he deceived and ran away from his master, and how he finally found safe haven in a commune of runaway slaves in Fort Blount."[43] The last part of the poem, included in the anthology and dedicated to Harlem of New York, is as follows:

> While my montage in Harlem
> Will show how freely Sambo lives.
>
> …Can mere words aim
> To relate truthfully
> How Sambo's life in Harlem
> Is blossoming with beauty? […]
>
> Thoughts leapt like deer and
> Hearts rose in the air:
> In Harlem! In Harlem!—
> You'll find black millionaires!
>
> Replace the harps, pick up the horns!

---

42 Vitalii Korotych, *Kurbatura iaitsia* (Kyiv: Molod', 1977), 20, 27–28.

43 Yohanan Petrovsky-Shtern, *The Anti-Imperial Choice: The Making of the Ukrainian Jew* (New Haven, CT: Yale University Press, 2009), 96–97. Chap. 2 of the monograph focused on the life and creative activity of Ivan Kulyk.

And play the bugles non-stop!
In Harlem! In Harlem!
The blacks are even cops! …

There blow hot winds
Down streets and avenues:
But most of all in Harlem—
There are black prostitutes. […]

… Let black
Join white
And white
Join black,
Let skyscrapers like masts
Arise from the dead bodies,
Let bruised heads in bunches
Hang above the shipyards.

But that's not from the Black Epos.
That's from the Red Epos.[44]

The text demonstrates various formal commitments to the epoch, such as cine-montage and montage of poetical rhythmic patterns, in addition to showing how enthusiasm for the alleged opportunities of the Harlem Renaissance were marred by reality—how "black millionaires" morphed into "black prostitutes." Kulyk plays here with the political semantics of colors—he mixes the black of skin and the red of blood to pronounce his verdict that blackness cannot find its true realization in New York without the red of the political Left. Another curious aspect seen in this poem is its aversion to exoticism—Kulyk mistrusts clichés about the dangerous yet sensual streets of Harlem—and as a result, he does not exoticize danger.

This political anxiety becomes more pronounced with time; thirty years later, a poem by Vadym Lesych establishes the contrast between the vision of Harlem as a place of exotic otherness and Harlem as a socially difficult locale of displacement:

They roam in white day
from one street to the next,

---

44 Ivan Kulyk, From "Black Epos," trans. Alexander Motyl, p. 31, 33 in this volume.

> so empty and sad,
> dragging black otherness,
> the same kind as we—
> gapers, poets, comedians,
> and those who, in worry,
> expect their burdensome motherhood.[45]

Lesych's compares the inhabitants of Harlem and his own kin—the poets and artists of Ukrainian New York—and finds two populations whose joy remains elsewhere. The topography of New York becomes a topography of global difference—it is pervaded by the sensations, memories, and projections from various "Old Countries."

In Yuri Kosach's poem we can see some similarities:

> thousands of arms like quivering cobras
> thousands of legs on the footpaths to heaven.
>
> o god with the yellow eyes
> o mother on the black donkey
> going to Egypt
> down the path with the falling stones
> down the difficult path of refugees
> hapless and unfree
> pass the black bread
> the bread that isn't sown
> the bread that isn't reaped
> the bread of heaven
> with the trees where the red-feathered
> cockatoo rocks.[46]

Again, we see an interplay with the colors red and black. However, this time black is not only the color of racial perception, it's also the color of black bread, the bread of the poor worldwide, and red is the color of memory and nostalgia, the color of the bird that sang in their abandoned country of origin.

---

45 Vadym Lesych, "Harlem: Day (III)," trans. Olga Gerasymiv and Jazlyn Kraft, p. 61 in this volume.

46 Yuri Kosach, "Manhattan, 103rd Street," trans. Ali Kinsella, p. 67 in this volume.

These two sentiments, empathy and awe, pervade Ukrainian poetry about Harlem. Ukrainian poets move closer to Harlem in different ways through their observations; Drach, for one, not only describes how he saves an exhausted black man on the subway, but how this encounter exemplified for him the whole social, political, and philosophical world of blackness—and how it can be approached through action and learning. One of the leading theoreticians of urban blackness in the twentieth century, James Baldwin, permeates the fabric of Drach's politically engaged text:

> Just two white guys who were brave
> Enough to enter his black ghetto—
> Suffering, isolated, and resisting.
> Caution! Stay and guard us!
> It's time to read James Baldwin
> To feel the African-American spirit
> Full of fetor and full of wind ...[47]

And if we follow Drach's invitation, when reading Baldwin we find these famous impassioned lines on New York:

> "Whoever is born in New York is ill-equipped to deal with any other city: all other cities seem, at best, a mistake, and, at worst, a fraud. No other city is so spitefully incoherent. Whereas other cities flaunt there history—their presumed glory—in vividly placed monuments, squares, parks, plaques, and boulevards, such history as New York has been unable entirely to obliterate is to be found, mainly, in the backwaters of Wall Street, in the goat tracks of Old and West Broadway, in and around Washington Square, and, for the relentless searcher, in grimly inaccessible regions of The Bronx."[48]

Ukrainian poets dared to experience and write about "the grimly inaccessible regions" of the city, both for their political agendas and their quest for identity.

---

47 Ivan Drach, "For Dmytro Pavlychko," trans. Ostap Kin and Ali Kinsella, p. 149, 151 in this volume.

48 James Baldwin, *Just Above My Head* (New York: New Dial, 1979), 227–228.

Broadway

The world knows many things about New York City—or thinks it does, at least. Due to the speedy globalization of recent decades, the list of commonly known toponyms is on the rise. Often, however, poets became rooted in one neighborhood, and did not try to explore beyond it—that is, to actively drift through the urban space. Occasionally, this happened because they felt alienated. Some authors stopped walking the city to concentrate on their areas of residence, for example, the East Village. This could have led to a relative unfamiliarity with the city and perhaps even a lack of interest in it. A Romanian émigré author once experienced something similar: "The writer, caught up in the shelter of solitude, does not have much time to wander about. His neighborhood is his world, the geography of his calendar." The author, however, hastens to add that New York City's streets "offer extraordinary spectacles wherever one is."[49]

The most popular toponyms, however, remain the same. One such example is, indisputably, Broadway. This road begins in the Bowling Green district of downtown Manhattan and stretches the length of the island for thirteen miles, continuing on for two additional miles in the Bronx; it then exits north of the city, where runs for another eighteen miles.

One example follows: an unidentified author that hides behind the pseudonym V. Rudeychuk—though, admittedly, this could be a real name—steps off Broadway into an area that might be called Greenwich Village nowadays. In his 1928 poem "New York," Broadway is a site of clear class divisions: "On West Broadway someone cries: / 'A bottle of beer, two of champagne, / Mademoiselle planted in the limousine.'"[50]

Yevhen Malanyuk, whose main corpus of poems about New York City was written during the poet's initial years in the city (namely, from 1949 to 1953), consistently associates Broadway with a canyon, a deep cleft between two cliffs. It is unlikely that the poet ever visited any canyons in the United States, and just as unlikely that he saw Berenice Abbott's photographs of New York in the 1930s.[51] The symbol of the canyon shows us that Malanyuk thought of Broadway as a nuanced locus of the city. One such depiction reads as follows: "In Manhattan's sunless creases, / In Broadway's canyon craziness / There is no blueness and no sun / -the trees don't rustle / -and space never breathes".[52]

---

49 Norman Manea, *The Fifth Impossibility* (New Haven, CT: Yale University Press), 322.
50 V. Rudeychuk, "New York," trans. Abbey Fenbert, p. 27 in this volume.
51 See, for example, Elizabeth McCausland and Berenice Abbott, *New York in the Thirties* (Mineola, NY: Dover Publications, 2013).
52 Yevhen Malanyuk, "New York Shorthand," trans. Alexander Motyl, p. 43 in this volume.

Broadway is also the place where times passes through something that may be described as a darkness roused out of dirt—or "smoke," to be more accurate: "And all the days that crisscross / Broadway's smoke-filled canyon".[53] Malanyuk also substitutes, or rather finds, a synonym for "canyon" in his poem "Thoughts," in which Broadway is an "abyss" constructed of "waves of stone and steel:" "An azure rectangle above Broadway's abyss / Waves of stone and steel. A sleepless haze."[54] In Malanyuk's poetry, Broadway becomes a dangerous and sublime natural phenomenon.

Yuri Kosach, a poet who belongs to a younger generation than Malanyuk, also moved to New York City after World War II, at the same time as Malanyuk. In his poem "Broadway," Kosach, too, offers a notion of an "abyss" in connection to Broadway, but in a somewhat different way: "you glide, glide like a dead-eyed idol, / along the abysses of faceless Broadway." Broadway here is a venue of various sorts of idols, along whom one is strolling, and the abysses (again) of the main New York streets are faceless. Closer to the end of his poem, while speaking of the city's probable and imagined destruction, one will remain with the street of Broadway: "You'll still have your canyons of streets, Broadway," and the city's heart will continue beating: "your still-stone, still-alive heart will beat."[55] In the other poem entitled "Ballad of Golden Broadway," Kosach remains faithful to the city that adopted him, or rather maybe the city he himself adopted, after his escape from post-war Europe. In what may be described as a conflicting depiction of the city, Broadway is portrayed as a river and a frigate. Golden Broadway moves along the street and the glimmering streetlights ("neon"); however, it is not known if they illuminate the street, since the street is already deserted: "So is she, blue-lashed Ophelia from the neon desert of Broadway." The poem's ending suggests that Broadway will still remain, and it seems that the author supports this continuation and and hopes that this area will thrive:

> Broadway still glows, the banquet continues
> But, though we may be mad, let's pass it by,
> Let's leave this horde of pirates, of scoundrels
> (May the screeching of their laughter hang in a haze!).
> We must pave the way to the wondrous places,

---

53 Yevhen Malanyuk, "Untitled," trans. Alexander Motyl, p. 47 in this volume.
54 Yevhen Malanyuk, "Thoughts," trans. Alexander Motyl, p. 49 in this volume.
55 Yuri Kosach, "Broadway," trans. Ali Kinsella, p. 73 in this volume.

Faster on the wings of the tempests!
Faster with the stars in spring![56]

Dima belongs to a completely different generation than both Malanyuk and Kosach. In her poem "Broadway in the Evening," the street is a location that collects all sorts of lights that originate from ads: "Ads, ads, ads… / Above us, below us, on all sides." However, the ads produce such a myriad of lights that there is no delight in encountering them: "You walk along Broadway / In the evening /And it starts to feel creepy / From all those colorful stains…"[57] Writing about the lights on Broadway is not a novel topic, but rather a continuous one spanning from decade to decade, from one generation of poets to another. For example, Lorca, too, pointed out that Broadway is full of colors and lights.

The way Abram Katsnelson perceived the city suggests yet another example of a poet-visitor and his relation with the city. For the poet, Broadway becomes a scene "illuminated by ads aglow" (here again the topic of lights and colorful ads emerges), where a lyrical character encounters a Jewish person "saved by God," but also with a "mouth split and splayed" that was "slashed in a concentration camp with a blade." For Katsnelson, who was born in a shtetl in what is now the Chernihiv region, the topic of Eastern European Jewishness becomes fairly significant right after his visit to New York and his presumable encounters, at least visual if not verbal, with Holocaust survivors.

Ukrainian Poets of New York and Their Virgils

For a number of poets from Eastern Europe, Ukrainian poets included, one of the possible ways to get to know the city and comprehend it was through the interlocutors: foreign poets whose poetry on the city of New York became available for reading. There are, for example, several of the most frequently encountered foreign poets whose poetry was of a certain scale for Ukrainian writers: the American poet Walt Whitman, the Spanish poet Federico Garcia Lorca, and the Soviet Russian poet Vladimir Mayakovsky.

Walt Whitman's relationship with Russian and Eastern European literatures takes its beginning sometime in the second half of the nineteenth century and becomes more and more intense in the early twentieth century,

---

56 Yuri Kosach, "Ballad of Golden Broadway," trans. Ali Kinsella, p. 85 in this volume.
57 Dima, "Broadway in the Evening," trans. Ostap Kin and Ali Kinsella, p. 133 in this volume

as he becomes a gradually popular poet first among Eastern European poets and then readers; his work was translated and re-printed into languages such as Czech, Polish, and Russian.[58] Whitman's influence is apparent for at least several generations of Ukrainian poets, some of them who visited, such as Drach, Korotych, and Kulyk, as well as for those who lived in New York City. Les Herasymchuk suggested that "[t]he peculiarity of Ukrainian Whitmanism is that it takes its beginning not from the translation, critics, but from direct or indirect borrowing of the aesthetic ideas of Walt Whitman."[59]

As early as in the 1922 poem "Speech," the futurist Mykhail Semenko declares the following:

Коли Уолт Уітмен вмер
(1892)
народився
я.[60]

[When Walt Whitman died / (1892) / I / was born].

According to Oleh S. Ilnytzkyj, by "[r]elating his own physical born with Walt Whitman's year of death, Semenko presents himself as if he had been a reincarnation of the renowned American."[61] Whitman becomes somewhat of an unrecognized and continuous Virgil for Ukrainian poets; they enjoyed the poet's poetics but, likely, he also became the one who made a bridge between the countries, between the literary traditions, even though not all visited the city. But what was probably one of the main things that attracted poets was how they saw the city (probably for one of the first times) through the poems of Walt Whitman, who himself was a passionate lover and appreciator of the city. "Whitman, though a native of the New York area, loved it and wrote of it with the zeal and zest usually found in those from elsewhere who have made

---

58 F. Lyra, "Whitman in Poland," and Stephen Stepanchev "Whitman in Russia." In *Walt Whitman and the World*, 295–299; 300–313. Gay Wilson Allen and Ed Folsom, eds. (Iowa City: University of Iowa Press, 1995).

59 Les' Herasymchuk, "Amerykans'kyi bard v Ukraini. Retseptsiia dorobku Volta Vitmena." *Sumno.com*. 26 July 2009. Available: http://sumno.com/article/amerykanskyj-bard-v-ukrajini/#_ednref41 (accessed on November 13, 2017).

60 Mykhail' Semenko, *Vybrani tvory*, Anna Bila, ed. (Kyiv: Smoloskyp, 2010), 149.

61 Oleh Il'nyts'kyi [Oleh S. Ilnytzkyj], "Ukrains'ka avanhardna poeziia: povernennia do chytacha." In *Ukrains'ka avanhardna poeziia (1910–1930-ti roky): antolohiia*, Oleh Kotsarev and Iuliia Stakhivs'ka, eds. (Kyiv: Smoloskyp, 2014), 8.

New York their chosen home."[62] Because of this fact, Walt Whitman became the American poet associated strongly with walking in the city, trying to understand the city on site, thinking very attentively about the city.[63]

The artist Louis Lozowick, once a student at an art school in Kyiv, wrote in his memoir about the first impressions of his stay in New York:

> "To me America would be the beginning of a new life; to others, a final resting place; to all, a plunge into the unknown. [...] We took the ferry and landed in Manhattan.[64] The uncertainty of a month's pilgrimage was over. I looked up and down at the unusual environment. The skyscrapers, which later formed the subject of so many of my pictures, now looked forbidding, breathed a chilly indifference. But just as new sights were an object of curiosity to me, so apparently was I an object of curiosity to others, to judge from the way everybody stared at me. I was dressed in one of those embroidered Ukrainian shirts with a high collar (made familiar in this country by the Russian ballet), its tails hanging over the trousers and a cord with tassels tied around the waist. My brother looked at the people staring at me, then looked at me and said, 'You'll need a new outfit.' My Americanization had begun."[65]

Lozowick arrived in New York in 1906, and by the end of his life had become a successful artist with a career in the United States. In the first half of the 1920s, his paths crossed with those of Mykola Tarnovsky; both attended the meetings of progressive socialist organizations based in New York. Tarnovsky arrived in New York just a few years after Lozowick, in the early 1910s, from a different part of what is now Ukraine, and felt terrified by the city he encountered after exiting his ferry from Ellis Island to Manhattan: "In front of me,

---

62 Henry M. Christman, ed. *Walt Whitman's New York: From Manhattan to Montauk* (Lanham, MD: New Amsterdam Books, 1989), xi.

63 The scholar of American New York suggests that the latter was putting together the "picture" of the city: "Whitman's impact on walking-round literature was vast, partly because his all-embracing, synthesizing persona helped organize the streets' random stimuli: what we now call the problem of 'sensory overload.'" [...] This gargantuan process of assimilation, engorging the world by looking at it and naming it, was fueled by the desire to make it everything in the cosmos" (Phillip Lopate, *Waterfront: A Journey Around Manhattan* [New York: Crown Publishers, 2004], 204).

64 Here, Lozowick is referring to himself and his brother.

65 Virginia Hagelstein Marquardt, ed. *Survivor from a Dead Age: The Memoirs of Louis Lozowick* (Washington, D.C.: Smithsonian Institution Press), 139–140.

on a certain distance, there was something similar to the stone woods. This spectacle was similar to jungles which I saw on a picture in the past."[66]

Federico Garcia Lorca spent less than a year in New York, namely, the period between June 1929 and March 1930. It has been speculated that the Spanish poet felt uneasy about drifting around the city and preferred to spend his time in Harlem, consciously restraining his personal geography of the city to his neighborhood of residence. Lorca is of great influence for many Ukrainian poets.

> "On arriving to New York, one feels overwhelmed, but not frightened. I found it uplifting to see how man can use science and technology to make something as impressive as a spectacle of nature. It is incredible. The port and the lights of the skyscrapers, easily confused with the stars, the millions of other lights, and the rivers of automobiles are a sight like no other on earth. Paris and London are two tiny villages compared with this vibrant, maddening Babel."[67]

Lorca's feeling of surprise upon first seeing the city is, probably, not of much surprise in itself. People coming from different parts of the world, including from Eastern Europe, also had something that might be called shock. For many poets coming from Ukraine, it was their first visit to a foreign country, their "first encounter with the racial and religious diversity of a democratic society" and perhaps more importantly, "their first frightening glimpse of urban crowds."[68]

I would like to compare this with the poetry of New York-based Ukrainian poets of the 1920s. How did they perceive and depict the same city that Lorca saw? The one, if not the only, possible way to depict the city for that generation was to look through a political lens; that is, to compare New York life with catastrophe and dehumanization, whereas Lorca, in 1928, viewed the city as a source, which helped him change his views and expand his outlook in order to notice what was around him. It may be assumed that Ukrainian poets of that epoch concentrated, rather, on economical nuances, using poetry as an

---

66 Mykola Tarnovs'kyi, *Pivstolittia za okeanom: spohady kolyshn'oho emihranta* (Kyiv: Molod', 1979), 28.

67 [Lorca's letter to his relatives from New York, June 28, 1928], in *Federico Garcia Lorca, Poet in New York*, Christopher Maurer, ed. (New York: Noonday Press, 1991), 202.

68 Christopher Maurer, "Introduction," in Federico Garcia Lorca, *Poet in New York* (New York: The Noonday Press, 1991), xi.

xlvi | New York Elegies

instrument of critique, a means to promote the socialist and communist ideas that their city, at that time, was full of. At the same time, for Lorca, the city was a profound aesthetic paradigm, both muse and material from which to create.

An entry from a 1952 notebook suggests that Yevhen Malanyuk, after having lived in the city and in its vicinity for approximately three years, still experienced considerable conflicting feelings toward the city and had issues with acceptance: "After crossing the Hudson River, in front of the New York panorama, you imagine yourself a Gulliver: all these buildings and the very structure of city reminded you of the buildings of white ants. [...] Here there is no place and could not be for an *homme libre*. Here you cannot feel the Human at all."[69]

In Lieu of a Conclusion

The overall intention of this anthology is to delineate Ukrainian poetry about New York City as a unique corpus of texts in its dynamic relationship with the other national poetries dedicated to this exciting city. It should be repeated, once again, that New York is a topos of strong attraction for the poets. Regardless of the poet's geographic origin and background, if this poet finds him or herself in New York, it will likely become a powerful source for—or of—astonishment, deliberation, and rejection. Looking attentively at the poems, beginning with work from the early 1920s and ending with poems from the mid-2010s, one observes a vibrant and ceaselessly dynamic use of language, with which the poets depict both the city's vivacious and grim sides.

With the intensive alteration of voices, views of the city underwent energetic change. This change lies at the center of this anthology's exploration. In the Ukrainian poetic tradition—and here I mean namely the tradition of urban poetry—the city has been a theme that has been crystalizing and defining its boundaries within said tradition. We may outline several ways to look at the city: abstractly, as often in the poems of those authors who never saw the city but not necessarily; concretely, as in the poems of the poets of the latest decades, where one is able see the city the way it was; and in the perspectives of social concern, which can be sharply discerned in the texts produced by the post-World War II generations of poets.

---

69 Ievhen Malaniuk, *Notatnyky: 1936–1968*, Leonid Kutsenko, ed. (Kyiv: Tempora, 2008), 116.

Ukrainian poets connected themselves to a powerful myth of New York, the myth of urban modernity and problematic vitality. The city of exiles and outsiders sees itself reflected in the mirror that newcomers and exiles created. By adding new voices and layers to this amalgam, it is possible to observe the expanded picture of this worldly poetic city. The Ukrainian poet connected, and continues to connect, to one the most radical urban myths in existence. As far back as 1923, the compilers of the then-first, as they claimed, "anthology of general city verse [on New York]" had suggested that "[a] great city is a great poem—not a poem by a dapper and correct versifier, but a poem by a Shakespeare, rough it may be and coarse at times, but filled with nobility and war, with the presence of all humanity."[70]

The present anthology allows its reader to observe how the poetic text of the Ukrainian New York developed over time while reflecting two realities at once: that of the city, which was its object of reflection, and that of poetic language, which was its instrument. The resulting collection has its masterpieces and curiosities, wonders and disappointments, but most crucially it testifies to the existence of a strong poetic attraction to a complex and significant urban site: New York. I hope that readers of this anthology will share with me the excitement that these poems emanate, paradoxically diverse despite being dedicated to one topic.

---

70 Garland Greever and Joseph M. Bachelor "Introduction," in *The Soul of the City: An Urban Anthology*, Garland Greever and Joseph M. Bachelor, eds. (Boston: Houghton Mifflin Company, 1923), x-xi.

Poems

Part I: 1920s–1930s

Михайль Семенко

ПРОЛЕТАРІ
УСІХ КРАЇН
ЄДНАЙТЕСЯ!

ЕЛЕКТРО

ВСТУП.

іскру
полум'я революції
думку-живчик
за океан.
пролети
мент-хвиля
темним дном атлянтики
лінія-дріт
далекий край.
в гамір
дротяних небодряціи
іскра-думка
атом огни-пожару
тенденція повстання-боротьби
не пускаю тебе
далі
останнього поверху.
і коли скажеш:
тісно—
в землю тебе пущу
де кружляє швидкий
метрополітен.

В

здіймемо гамір
ланцюгами
гір!

СЛУХАЙТЕ!

(циркулярно).

Москва—Владивосток—Гонолулу—Сан-Франциско—Чікаго—Ню-Йорк—Лондон—Париж—Берлін—Варшава—Київ

(циркулярно).

електричною ниткою
духу криці
обмотую камінь
взліво й дим
нолею людини знаволеної,
сталевий птах кине оком
на горизонти міст.
іскра зворушить огни серць,
дляться золи суцільна
улиці тунелі й
потягами кам'яниць.
од міста до міста проллеться хвиля
дзвони й сурми новітніх бійців.
сонце нигнино на руїну
піде клич з континенту на
континент.

РИМ

РУДА
УД РУ ДУ
ДА
А ДУР

О

барикади
в лавах хребтів
на спинах!

ПАРИЖ

АЕРО

МОСКВА

Михайль Семенко. Поезомалярство. „Каблепоема". Картка № 2.

Mykhail Semenko

2

ELECTRO

INTRO.
spark
flame of the revolution
thought-pulse
across the ocean.
flies
moment-wave
by dark depths of the atlantic
line-wire
distant land.
into the noise
of wire skyscrapers
spark-thought
atom of fire-blaze
tendency of riot-fight
I won't let you
past
the final floor.
and when you say:
it's too tight
I'LL LET YOU TO THE GROUND
where hovers the fast
metropolitan.
LISTEN!
(circularly).
Moscow-Vladivostok-Honolulu
San-Francisco-Chicago-New
York-London-Paris-Berlin
Warsaw-Kyiv
(circularly).
with an electric thread
of steel soul
I wind stone
iron and smoke
freed by the will of man.
a steel bird will cast an eye
at cities' horizons.
the spark moves the flames of hearts.
a continuous will pours
streets tunnels and
trains of tenements.
from city to city will flow
a wave of cries and trumpets of the latest
warriors.
the sun will look on the ruin
the word will go from continent to
continent.

MOSCOW

U

*Let's make noise
with chains
of mountains!*

ROME

**ORE
R [ORE] R
ERO**

O

*Barricades
in rows of spines
on backs!*

PARIS

AERO

Mykhail Semenko. Poetrypainting   *"Cablepoem". Card 2. 1921*

Translated by Ostap Kin and Marlow Davis

**ТРОЩІТЬ
В ЧЕРЕПКИ
КАПИТАЛІЗМ!**

МАШИНА.

переможці
ми.
земля людині.
ударники
ми
мірнемо суходолами
кладемо материк
на материк
ми можем ще більше!
мрівняєм
вдаговища рік!
сполучим
бассейни каналами!
масиви гір
продинамітим
і видобудем
корисну руду.
пустим машину
по землі й
під землею
і під
дном світових океанів.
завтра:
будем як дома
в системі
планет.
сьогодні:
витиснем олію землі
мішень трудових
куль
землі.
погинем шахти!
гасло:
копальні.
завдання:
машина титан,
наш брат
сміливий і талановитий,
поволі
геній
мруть.
швидче—разом
КОНТИНЕНТИ
швидче—разом
РОБІТНИКИ
машина
жде!

НЮ-ИОРК

З — *переллїть бассейны океанів і морів!*

АНТРАЦИТ

Л — *вимотаєм плянету щоб сполучить світи!*

ІНТЕРНАЦІОНАЛ

З — *глиби хребтів падають до ніг!*

О — *бігунови кола стиснуть поверхнь подій!*

Михайль Семенко, Повзомалярство. „Кабліпоема". Картка № 6.

SMASH CAPITALISM INTO BITS!

M A C H I N E.

winners

are we.

THE EARTH FOR MAN

shock workers

are we.

we measure the dry land

we place continent

upon continent.

WE CAN DO STILL MORE!

let's level

mouths of rivers!

let's unite

basins with canals!

massifs of mountains

let's dynamite away

and exctract

useful ore!

let's release machinery

upon the land and

below the land

and below

the depth of the world's oceans.

TOMORROW:

we shall be at home

in the solar

system.

TODAY:

let's squeeze oil from the land

the target of working

bullets

is land.

let's deepen the shafts!

MOTTO:

mines.

GOAL:

A machine titan.

our brother

courageous and talented.

geniuses

slowly

die.

faster–together

CONTINENTS

faster–together

WORKERS

the machine

awaits

N E W Y O R K

Z *Pour out the oceans into the seas!*

ANTHRACITE

L *Let's unwind the planet in order to unite worlds!*

INTERNATIONAL

Z *The masses of ranges are falling to our feet!*

O *Running circles will compress the surfaces of events!*

6

Mykhail Semenko. Poetrypainting.   "Cablepoem". Card 6. (1921)

Translated by Ostap Kin and Marlow Davis

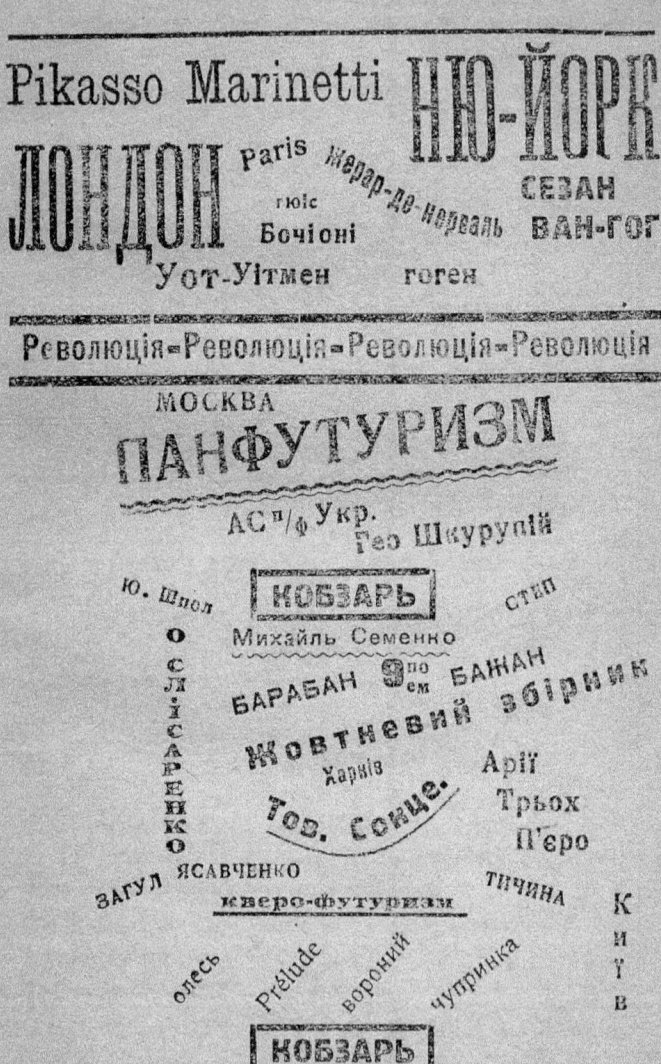

Picasso   Marinetti   **NEW-YORK**

LONDON Paris

guis   GERARD-DE-NERVAL   **CEZANNE**

Boccioni   **VAN-GOGH**

Walt-Whitman   gauguin

Revolution-Revolution-Revolution-Revolution

MOSCOW

PANFUTURISM

AS P/F Ukr.

Geo Shkurupiy

Yu. Shpol

O   STEPPE

S   **KOBZAR**

L   Mykhail Semenko

I

S   **9** PO EMS   BAZHAN

A   DRUM   **Anthology**

R   **October**

E   Arias

N   Kharkiv   Of Three

K   **Comrade Sun**   Pierrots

O

ZAHUL   YA.SAVCHENKO   TYCHYNA

QUERO-FUTURISM   K

Y

oles   Prélude   vorony   chuprynka   I

V

KOBZAR

Taras Shevchenko

"System". 10 July 1922. Kyiv.   **Poetrypainting**

Translated by Ostap Kin and Marlow Davis

Решта

I.

Нахмурило брови
    сизі брови над київом
ще на сезон зоставлено
    ласий кусок
і питає поет розгублено
     а як же «убий його»
       і як же владивосток
     а як же париж і лондон
       чикаго і ню-йорк
     і знову латані вітрини хрещатика
      рейтерська
        і кава
          і дощ
прострель мене прикнопнутого
    на меридіані київському
прострель мене наскрізь стріло віків!

3.X.1922, Київ

The Rest

I.

The eyebrows furrowed,
  the blue-grey eyebrows above Kyiv
the tender morsel is set aside
  for one more season
and a poet asks in bewilderment
  what's with this "kill him"
   and what about Vladivostok
  what about Paris and London
   Chicago and New York
  and again the mended showcases on Khreshchatyk
   Reiterska Street
    and coffee
     and the rain
shoot me buttoned up
  on the Kyiv meridian
shoot right through me, arrow of ages!

October 3, 1922, Kyiv

Translated by Ostap Kin and Ali Kinsella

Олекса Слісаренко

Уот Уітмен

Я чоловік
Такий звичайний, що аж смішно —
Ріка кришталева у смердючих берегах.
Віки
Шелестять наді мною крилами.
Тремтіння і жах
Перетоплюю на сміливість у своїх гамариях,
Слухаю шуми вітру, машин і
дихання коханої женщини;
Бачу хмари, землю, димарі, звірів і людей;
Мацаю речі, нюхаю запахи.
Я такий звичайний, що аж смішно —
І день мій розцвітаю, як лотос.

<1923>

Oleksa Slisarenko

Walt Whitman

I'm a man
So simple it's funny—
The river flows crystal-clear between reeking banks.
The ages
Rustle their wings above me.
I melt down
Shivering and horror into courage in my forges,
I listen to the noise of the wind and cars, and
The breathing of a loving woman,
I see clouds, the land, chimneys, animals, and people;
I touch things; I inhale smells.
I am so simple it's funny—
And my day blossoms like a lotus.

<1923>

Translated by Ostap Kin and Ali Kinsella

Микола Тарновський

Subway

Під землею гуркотіння —
Вічний клекіт, шум…
Вогко… Тухло… Темно… Сум!
Входять люди, а склепіння
Висне понад ними;
Входять сходами брудними —
В пітьму, мов на глум!

«Собвей» — мов ті катакомби,
станції — мов олтарі;
всюди виломи і щомби —
мов казкові упирі!
Пруться люди до вагонів —
Спішно, вперто… (це життя?)
Мов у пащу лізуть смерті —
Без надії, без пуття…
І потягне їх той поїзд —
Десь на інші «олтарі»!..

Зяють злі і чорні пащі —
Під домами вшир і вглиб…
Не один за це трудящий
Марно смертю тут погиб!

1924

Mykola Tarnovsky

Subway

Rumbling down below—
Eternal roar, scream …
Humid… Rancid… Wretched… Grief!
Down the people go,
The vaults hanging overhead;
Down they go by dirty steps—
Into the darkness, taunting them!

The subway is like the crypts,
The stations are like altars;
Everywhere pits and zombies
like fantastical monsters!
The people push their way to the cars—
Impatient, stubborn … (what life is this?)
Like they're climbing into death's jaws—
To no avail, and hopeless
And the train drags them—
Somewhere to other "altars!"

The black and evil jaws gape
Under the houses' depth and breadth
For this, more than one worker
died a pointless death.

1924

Translated by Abbey Fenbert

На П'ятій Авеню

Декорації! Пишні окраси!
Сліпнуть очі — блискуча краса!
З вікон лізуть прерізні гримаси:
— Небеса! Небеса! Небеса!

Тротуари — як ріки … Громадно
Декорації ходять живі …
Та зовсім вже, зовсім непринадно, —
Наче мумії ті вікові!

На обличчя дивись і дивуйся:
Де ж та сила? І де та краса? —
Мов примари з надхмарних екскурсій:
— Небеса! Небеса! Небеса!

Розмальовано все це завзято …
Це «артисти» (на щастя — не всі!);
Так багато «артистів», багато —
Та нема в них живої душі!

1927

On Fifth Avenue

The scenery! Lush decorations!
The eyes go blind—beautiful brilliance!
Through the windows peer all kinds of faces
Heavens! Heavens! Heavens!

The sidewalks are like rivers
The living decorations go in crowds
Such unattractive figures
As if wrapped in ancient shrouds!

Look at their faces and be amazed
Where is that beauty? And where is that strength?
Like unearthly wandering shades
—Heavens! Heavens! Heavens!

All of this is painted fervently,
These con artists (happily, not all)
So many such artists, many
And in not one a living soul!

1927

Translated by Abbey Fenbert

У місті, де жив Уот Уітмен

У місті, де жив Уот Уітмен,
Гуля світовий сатана Мефістофель —
Модерний, новітній …
Гудуть іще скрізь катастрофи
Всесвітні,
А тут — світова карузель …

Уот Уітмен! Поміж будівель
Ще є вулиці ті рухливі,
Куди ти колись походжав,
Де ти приставав з бідаками,
Що їх ще так повно усюди …

У місті, де жив Уот Уітмен,
Я хочу сміятися сміхом тим віщим,
Що, ось, вже наповнює груди
Життям динамітним,
Що вибухне й місто розбудить …
Розбудить? Здригне?
Чи здригне — я питаю —
Закурене, сковане місто?..
Розбудить! Я знаю!
Я хочу сміятися сміхом віщим,
Бо, ось, він уже напирає,
Вже вибухне скоро!
                    Дивіться!
Мефісто —
Обтислі штанці,
І шабля блискуча при боці, —
Як лицар ступає …
У нього ж тут завжди на оці
Залюблений Фауст!

О Фаусте юноподібний!
О, Фаусте! Ти — як юнак!
В тобі закохалась, напевно,
Сліпа Маргарита;
Вона закохалась не менше,

In the City Where Walt Whitman Lived

In the city where Walt Whitman lived,
the earthly devil Mephistopheles roams
Modern, new…
Earthly catastrophes still drone
Everywhere
And here—the carousel of the world

Walt Whitman! Among the buildings
There are still those lively streets
Where you once strolled,
Where you stood by the poor,
Who still fill those streets.

In the city where Walt Whitman lived,
I want to laugh with prophetic laughter
It is already filling my chest
With dynamite
That will explode and wake the city…
Will it rouse the city? Shake it?
Will it shake it? I ask,
This smoke-filled, shackled city?
It will wake up! I know!
I want to laugh with prophetic laughter
For now it keeps pressing, pressing
And it will soon explode!
                          Look!
Mephisto—
In his tight-fitting trousers
And a shining saber at his side
He steps in like a knight…
And in his eye, as ever,
The Enthralled Faust!

O youthful Faust!
O Faust! You are like a boy!
She fell in love with you, certainly,
Blind Margarita;
She fell in love no less

Як ти закохався у ній…
Безумний ти! Стій!
Усе це кохання — омана,
Усе це кохання — брехня!..
Мефісто тут паном…
Надармо ти ждеш того дня,
Щоби повінчатися з нею:
Тебе напоїв він брехнею —
Гидкий мефістофель! —
І ти, як подертий пантофель,
Не станеш вже новим…
І юності вже не розбудиш,
І щастя-життя не здобудеш…
Старого ніхто не поновить —
Життя не повернеш назад:
Ти мусиш умерти ганебно
Від кулі юнацької — там, з барикад…
Старого ніхто не поверне назад!
А гордий Мефісто,
Що крутить тобою вперед і назад,
Втече з барикад!
Та місто,
Що в ньому жив Уітмен,
Пародить живих юнаків,
Яких оновляти не треба,
Бо вічно будуть молоді
І вічно закохані в правду —
У дійсну уже Маргариту —
І так зустрічатимуть сонце.

Я хочу сміятися сміхом тим віщим,
Бо ось він бухне динамітно
І станеться те, що повинно,
Що мчиться і мчиться невпинно,
Мов ті карузелі…
Відродиться місто —
Старий розірветься пантофель,
Безрадний казитись буде Мефістофель.

1928

Than you fell in love with her…
You Fool! Stop!
All this love is a delusion
All this love is a lie
Mephisto is lord here…
In vain you wait for the day to marry her
He has made you drunk with lies
Vile Mephistopheles!
And you, like an old torn slipper,
Will never be new again…
And you will never revive your youth,
And you will never find joy in life…
The old cannot be made new
You cannot get your life back
You must die in shame
From youth's bullets—from that barricade,
the old cannot be turned back!
But proud Mephisto,
Who twists you back and forth,
Flees from the barricade!
And the city,
In which Whitman lived,
Will give birth to living youths,
Who do not need to be renewed,
For they will be forever young
And forever love the truth
Love the real Margarita
And so they will welcome the sun.

I want to laugh with prophetic laughter
For here it will burst like dynamite
And it shall be as it should be
That which rushes and rushes incessantly,
Like these carousels…
A city will be reborn
That old torn slipper
Mephistopheles, helpless, will rage.

1928

Translated by Abbey Fenbert

Касандрин

Times Square

Чудесний нюйоркський «Таймс-сквер»,
Гордість американської ночи!
Від реклям, орнаментів й світел
Сліпнуть очі.

Розсілися тут домо-велетні кругом,
Між ріжнобарвним електро-промінням…
Ані пяді землі не пустує даром —
Стогне під ногами, колесами й камінням…

Тисячі, тисячі… Море голів!..
Авто-машини, машини, машини…
Плинуть вгору, плинуть долів,
І кінця немає за ними.

Блиском, багатством вітрини забиті,
Розкішшю дихають шпари…
Чи є ще місце на нашім світі
Цьому до пари?

Єс, чудесний «Таймс-сквер»
Гордість американської ночи!
Та в грудях віддих спер…
Дихати в нім нема чим.

Убожество духа страшенне тут;
Й не шукай душевного тут зілля…
Як свойого ти не хоч стратити,
То втікай, друже, скоріш звідсілля!

<1924>

Kasandryn

Times Square

New York's wondrous Times Square
Pride of the American night!
The eyes go blind
From the ads, ornaments and lights.

Between polychrome electric beams
The skyscrapers have sat down
Not the smallest piece of soil goes bare
Wheels and stones groan underground

Automobiles, mobiles, mobiles…
Thousands, and thousands… a sea of heads!
They course through hills, through valleys
And it never ends.

Windows overflow with glitter and wealth
The chinks breathe opulence
Is there a place in all the world
That compares to this?

There it is, wondrous Times Square
Pride of the American night!
And in our chests, stifled air
Too stale to breathe.

Terrible poverty of the soul
Do not seek spiritual healing here…
If you do not wish to lose your own
Flee this place quickly, my dear!

<1924>

Translated by Abbey Fenbert

М. Пільний

Вже досить

Ню Йорк тремтить,
Горить огнями.
Женуть зміями
Елевейтери…
 Вперед все мчить…
А хмародери гінко
Підняли у блакить
Вершки.
 Так стрімко, стрімко.

——————

 І розкіш ватою м'якою
 Обвила клуби банкірів
 Хіба ж для них є смішною
 Похмура нужда злидарів?..
Ха-ха! Гелгоче хмільно глум…
А вікнами в акорд
Влетів нервовий міста шум
(Хтось… журиться за «борт»)
Вже досить щастя ситих!
Опаде золота луска.
Бо йдуть в контраст юрби прибитих,
Що хліба жебрають куска.

21.I.1928, Ню Йорк

M. Pilny

Enough Already

New York shakes,
Blazing with lights.
Elevators, snake-like,
Drive us…
    Forward we all race.
And the skyscrapers have sharply
Stretched their tips
Into the sky.
    So rapidly, rapidly.

    And in soft cotton, luxury
    Has wrapped the clubs of bankers
    Do they really find funny
    The dreary needs of beggars?
Haha! The drunken taunt crows…
And so the nervous city noise
Flew in through the windows
(Someone…has leapt overboard)
Enough fortune for the fat ones, already!
The golden scale descends.
For counter go the downtrodden crowds
scrounging for a piece of bread.

January 21, 1928, New York

Translated by Abbey Fenbert

В. Рудейчук

Ню Йорк

Мури, каміння, вежі ...
Як шпилі гір
Піднялись над землею, —
Піднялись аж до хмар,
І там вгорі немов плетуть
Таємну казку ... з наших
Славою ... оспіваних століть.
А тут? — Вдолині — цілісенький вулкан ...
Як в пеклі Данта ...
Свист, гудіння, крик ...
Над землею — землею і під землею,
Як буря филями на океані,
І дим, і дим ...
Тікає поміж немитими мурами
І небо займається огнем
На західнім бродвею ...
Хтось кричить:
«Бутельку пива, дві — шампан,
Мадам-мозель всадити в лемозийн»
І далі сміх, перфума, дим ...
Танка під музику гуляють ...
А насподі? —
На чотирьох цілісеньких боках
Зчорнілі, чорні береги
І люди, люди ...
Жиють і дихають отут
Не у вежах, не у палатах,
А в малих полупаних хлівах.
На чотирьох або п'ятьох поверхах,
І плахтою холодною мряка,
Вкриває сплячий океан ...
Ах!..
А ось — людське якесь єство,
Аж страх!

V. Rudeychuk

New York

Walls, stones, towers…
Like the spires of mountains
They rose above the earth—,
Rose all the way to the clouds,
And there in the mountains as if weaving
A secret tale… of our glory
Of our celebrated centuries.
And here?—in the valley—an entire volcano
As in Dante's Inferno…
A whistle, hum, scream…
Above the ground—on the ground and underground
As a storm of waves upon the ocean
Smoke and more smoke…
Escapes between the unwashed walls
And the sky is enflamed
On West Broadway someone cries:
"A bottle of beer, two of champagne,
Mademoiselle planted in the limousine"
And then laughter, perfume, smoke
Dancing to the music they go.
And on the bottom—?
On all four sides
Blackened, black shores
All the people, people…
They live and breathe here
Not in towers, not in palaces
But in small, shattered pens.
On four or five floors,
and the sleeping ocean covers them
with a blanket of cold mist…
Ah!…
What horror!
But look here—some kind of human creature
Lies silently, dying of hunger

На сходах під хлівами
Мовчки лежить, у голоді конає.
І спашений банкір
На «Волл-стрит» золото перебирає…
А на статуї «Свободи»
Тільки гніздо і горобці
Почвіркують…
У грудях, руках і голові.

* * *

Мури, каміння, вежі…
Як шпилі гір,
Піднялись над землею, —
Піднялись аж до хмар,
І там вгорі немов плетуть
Таємну казку… з наших
Славою… оспіваних століть.

15.XI.1928, Ню Йорк

On the stairs near the cowsheds.
And the banker, fattened up,
Sorts the gold on Wall Street
And on the Statue of Liberty
Only a nest, and sparrows
Chirp...
On her chest, arms and head.

* * *

Walls, stones, towers...
Like the spires of mountains
They rose above the earth—,
Rose all the way to the clouds,
And there in the mountains as if weaving
A secret tale... of our glory
Of our celebrated centuries.

New York, November 15, 1928

Translated by Abbey Fenbert

Іван Кулик

Чорна Епопея (уривок)

Апофеоз

Самбо в Гарлемі

Ми звикли кадрами ударними
Величне славити й нове —
Я ж монтуватиму, як в Гарлемі
Самбо звільнений живе.

Хіба словами скажеш марними,
Хіба про те розповіси,
Як Самбове життя у Гарлемі
Буяє, сповнене краси?

Війна війнула хмарами
На дальні горизонти:
Охочих таки в Гарлемі
Знайшлося йти на фронт.

Над Іпрами, над Марнами,
Крошило нас недурно:
Своя ж вітчизна в Гарлемі,
Вільна й культурна.

Возами санітарними
Тягли оцупки ваші —
Зате знайшли у Гарлемі
Таке, що аж-аж-аж!

Думки стрибнули сарнами,
Серце аж ген в етері:
У Гарлемі! У Гарлемі! —
Навіть чорні мільйонери!

Не арфами — фанфарами!
Ревіть! Ревіть! Валторни!
У Гарлемі! У Гарлемі!
І полісмени! Чорні!

Ivan Kulyk

From the poem *Black Epos*

Apotheosis

Sambo in Harlem

We celebrate in film
The great and new with striking clips—
While my montage in Harlem
Will show how freely Sambo lives.

Can mere words aim
To relate truthfully
How Sambo's life in Harlem
Is blossoming with beauty?

Beyond the far horizon
There gathered clouds of war
And many men in Harlem
For the front did volunteer.

At Ypres and on the Marne
They hit us really hard:
Our homeland is in Harlem,
It's free and quite cultured.

The sanitary wagons
Carted your remains—
Meanwhile back in Harlem
Life was hey-hey-hey!

Thoughts leapt like deer and
Hearts rose in the air:
In Harlem! In Harlem!—
You'll find black millionaires!

Replace the harps, pick up the horns!
And play the bugles non-stop!
In Harlem! In Harlem!
The blacks are even cops!

А ввечері — рекламами
Гергочуть спрагло гони.
І ліхтарі у Гарлемі
Вовтузяться червоні;

Алеями бульварними —
Жагучі суховії:
Найбільше ж є у Гарлемі —
Чорних повій.

І юрбляться отарами
Чепуруни тендітні;
Ще більше є у Гарлемі
У чорних — чорних злиднів.

І де-не-де примарними
Шматками суне сумнів,
Що 'дним криваві в Гарлемі,
І іншим — злотні струмені;

Що, може, і програли ми
На Марні й під Верденом,
Що, може, треба в Гарлемі
Нових боїв злиденним,

Щоб клич новий у Гарлемі
На світ
Прокричали
Антени:

Щоб чорний
Разом з білим
На білого
Разом з чорним,
Щоб ледве з мертвого тіла
Хмарочоси продерли щогли,
Щоб голови рясно над реями
Звисали потовченими гронами…

Та це вже — не з Чорної Епопеї, —
Це — з Червоної.

1929

The evening signs of neon
Are hungry for arousing.
The lit street lamps in Harlem
Are red from their carousing.

There blow hot winds
Down streets and avenues:
But most of all in Harlem—
There are black prostitutes.

And crowds there do assemble
Of dandies tender and soft;
But more there is in Harlem
Black poverty quite oft.

And then appear the phantoms
Of doubt and questioning,
Cause some got blood in Harlem,
And some got golden rings.

Perhaps we lost the Marne
And the battle of Verdun,
Perhaps the fight in Harlem
Must poverty take on.

Let the new cry in Harlem
Be carried
To the world by
Antennas:

Let black
Join white
And white
Join black,
Let skyscrapers like masts
Arise from the dead bodies,
Let bruised heads in bunches
Hang above the shipyards.

But that's not from the Black Epos.
That's from the Red Epos.

1929

Translated by Alexander Motyl

Part II: 1940s–1980s

Євген Маланюк

* * *

Ані вершин, ані низин,
Що зрошені в веселих водах, —
Сумне ристалище машин
Та мстива, зраджена природа,

Та небо, що його безкрай
Покинув Бог.
             І у повітрі
Асфальту й нафти злий коктайль
Розносять бісенята хитрі.

І чад стоповерхових скель
Обапол уличних каньйонів —
Шляхи безрадісних пустель
Для безнадійних перегонів.

Тут згашено життя і дух,
І злобно визволено атом.
І чоловік навік потух,
І суду жде земля заклята.

30.VII.1949

Yevhen Malanyuk

* * *

There are no mountains, there are no fields,
There are no frolicsome waters,
There's but the sad charge of automobiles
And the vengeance of betrayed nature,

And a sky without future
Forsaken by God.
   The vile air is heavy
With an oily asphalt mixture
That wily imps spread gleefully.

And skyscraper cliffs tower
Above street canyons in the air—
These deserts are somber,
They stage races of despair.

Here life and spirit are suppressed,
As the evil atom runs free.
Forever mankind is quite dead,
And judged one day this cursed land will be.

July 30, 1949

Translated by Alexander Motyl

Одного дня

Димний день. Продзижчала підземка зловісно і лунко.
Коло днів замикається ще раз розла́дом наснаг.
І от берег ізнову …
                    І знову гірким поцілунком
Починається, може, остання, остання весна.

Тихий присмерк очей — золотіє в них лагідний вечір,
Материнське є щось у завчасній оцій сивизні,
Та як юно тремтять ці крихкі, як у дівчини, плечі
І уста — ніби вперше розхилені взустріч весні!

І ось дим прорізає несміливий промінь. І чудом —
День спалахує сяйвом, і сяйвом стає сивизна.
… І зникає цей го́род страшний, як нечиста облуда
… І в очах молодистих з'являється вічна весна.

25.X.1950

One Day

A day of smoke. The subway's loud and ominous.
The days come full circle, desire is lacking.
Here's the shore again…
                              And again a bitter kiss
Begins what may be the very last spring.

In the silent twilight of eyes, the gentle evening turns golden,
Graying prematurely, this hair has a mothering quality,
While girlish shoulders tremble like fragile children,
And, anticipating spring, eager lips open expectantly!

A hesitant ray severs the smoke. And miraculously
The day shines radiantly, as grayness becomes radiance.
… And there vanishes this unclean and evil city
… While spring eternal arises in youthful glances.

October 25, 1950

Translated by Alexander Motyl

Дні

Ти гинеш, гинеш разом з Нею,
Самотний гасне спів.

Ширяла юність орлім клектом
Нади височінню днів,
Аж ось вузький каньйон Бродвею,
Де сліпнеш над чужим проєктом
І гасиш жар і гнів.

Ґнітить каміння поверхове
І тисне як тягар.
… І все ж ти знаєш: ти не бранець,
Ти носиш віщий дар.
В тобі однім гримить Бетговен,
З тобою бачиться вибранець
Нещадних муз — Едґар.

1951

Days

As you die, as with Her you pass away,
A lonely song turns to haze.

As youth hovers like an eagle's cries
High above the heights of days,
There snakes a canyon, Broadway,
Where foreign notions blind your eyes
As you extinguish heat and rage.

The stony surface saddens
and forces you to the tar.
… And yet you know you're not broken,
As the gifts of prophets are yours.
In you alone thunders Beethoven,
And only you meet the man chosen
By the merciless muses—Edgar.

1951

Translated by Alexander Motyl

Ньюйоркські стенограми

М. Мухинові

І от життя веде криву
На злих координатах авеню і стрітів.

1.

В безсоняшних щілинах Мангаттану,
В каньйоні божевільного Бродвею
Ніколи — синява і сонце
        — шум дерев
        — і подих простору.

Ти, дню важкий,
Ти йдеш так мляво,
Все спотикаючись на перешкодах —
        — заснуть — заснуть.
А старість усміхається єхидно.
І наляга велика втома дня.

О ноче, що надходиш невблаганно!

... А там,

Далеко-далеко,
Через океан, моря і гори,
За руїнами вбогої Европи —
        — В лісах зеленої Шумави —
                — Сольвейґ!

    Її далекий спів,
    Що ледве вгадується,
    Ледь бринить.

2.

Я знаю, що надходить час — скориться
І примириться. Тяжко це й незвично.
Ще не проіржавіла в мені іскриста криця,
Ще не змішалося в мені дочасне й вічне.

Ще в серці зморенім горить мета.

New York Shorthand

To Mykhaylo Mukhyn

And so life's ugly curves
Are plotted on streets and avenues.

1.

In Manhattan's sunless creases,
In Broadway's canyon craziness
There is no blueness and no sun
          —the trees don't rustle
          —and space never breathes.

You, sluggish day,
You walk so slowly,
Constantly stumbling—
          —sleep—sleep.
As old age smiles maliciously
And life's exhaustion settles in.

O night that comes relentlessly!

... While over there,

Far, far away,
Beyond the oceans, seas and mountains,
Beyond wretched Europe's ruins—
          —Amidst Šumava's woods of green—
                    —Is Solveig!

  Her distant song,
  Almost unremembered,
  Is hardly heard.

2.

I know it's time to acquiesce
and to submit. That's hard and not my way.
My gleaming steel has yet to rust,
Eternity has yet to conquer my today.

My heart's ambitions have yet to die.

3.

... Коли спадає смерк,
    Запалюють вогні, —
    В старих провулках Бруклину брудного
    З-за рогу
    Раптом:
        — Постать у крилатці.
    Крават, як ворон, вп'явсь в охрипле горло,
    Налляті алькоголем тьмаві очі,
    Скуйовджене волосся _____
        То — безумний
          Едґар
    Вихаркує мені зітлілим перегаром
      Одне — єдине слово:
        Nevermore.

І тане в електричнім смерку,
    І зникає.

1952–1953

3.

… When dusk falls,
   When the lights go on,
   In filthy Brooklyn's ancient alleys
   From 'round a corner
   There suddenly appears:
           —A figure in a cloak.
   A raven-cravat clutching his hoarse throat,
   His dead eyes dulled by alcohol,
   His tousled hair———
           It's mad Edgar
   Spiritedly spitting at me
   A single word:
       Nevermore.

He melts away in the dusk electric.
   And disappears.

1952–1953

Translated by Alexander Motyl

* * *

I свічкою осяяний намет
По спеці цілоденної роботи
1944

Ні, не пустеля і намет,
Де ввечері святий спочинок, —
Ось знов любови дикий мед
І лиш пекучі сни про сина,

І самота — глуха жона,
Що доля повінчала з нею,
І дні, що їх перетина
Закурений каньйон Бродвею.

9.VI.1953

* * *

> And the candle lights the tent
> after a full day's hot work
>   1944

No, neither desert, nor tent
Provides nighttime's sacred sleep—,
Once more it's love's wild scent
And dreams of my son quite sweet,

And the deaf wife of loneliness
That fate bestowed on me, her man,
And all the days that crisscross
Broadway's smoke-filled canyon.

June 9, 1953

Translated by Alexander Motyl

Думи

І зламалось. І вже не зростити, ні склеїть.
Дні проходять, як риби на темному дні.
Прямокутник блакиті в проваллі Бродвею
Хвилі каменю й криці. Безсонні вогні.

Мертвий ідол машини явив підлюдину —
Суміш робота й малпи, механіки й зла.
Як навчатися маєш — забути — Єдину?
Розрубати тугу пуповину вузла?

Шкутильгатимуть роки — слизгава дорога.
Гуркотітиме вибухом проклятий вік.
Будеш бачити, як — без Природи і Бога —
Повертатиме в прах Чоловік.

21.VIII.1954

Thoughts

It finally broke. And it can't be fixed.
Like fish in the deep pass the days.
An azure rectangle above Broadway's abyss
Waves of stone and steel. A sleepless haze.

The mechanical idol of death bore a subhuman—
A cross between machine and evil, monkey and robot.
How should you study—or forget—the One?
How should the tightly tied knot be cut?

The years will limp down a slippery course.
Loud blasts will rock this cursed century.
Without Nature and God as his source—
You'll see Man become ashes, verily.

August 21, 1954

Translated by Alexander Motyl

Вадим Лесич

Нью-йоркські строфи

Квадратами площі вирують
І ринуть у струмені вулиць,
Впадають камінні в жару юрб,
Мов холоднокровні акули.

І тонуть в їх з'їжених пащах,
Що клацанням навстяж розверсті,
— заклятi у речі призначень
живі, перекровлені жертви,

аж сковзько хитнуться асфальти
у репаний ромб тротуарів
— у перспективах і звалах
блискучих і рвучих аварій.

Ідуть і гримлять у стоходах
трамваї і авта, і люди,
риштовання — чола підводять
у лябіринти споруди.

Поглинули простір пливучий
Розкриті синіючі вікна, —
Лиш — сходи, кружґанки, поруччя
— монументальність камінна.

У хмари незримо вросли ви
стрункі, непорушні, холодні —
будівлі картаті щасливих,
задивлені в сизі безодні.

В очах ваших вікон мінливих
не блимне в лету голубинім
окрилений кульбаби привид
над мармуром білого крину.

І вранці, у білім тумані,
не блисне крізь просвіт — тривога,
що десь в бурунах океанів
затоплений юности спогад.

Vadym Lesych

New York Verses

Squares rage and gush
Down the streams of the avenues
They flow, stony, into the heat of crowds,
Like cold-blooded sharks.

And inside their wiredrawn jaws
That are so wide, spread by clinging victims
drowning, bloody, yet still alive—
cursed into things of a purpose

and asphalt will shake here, unstable
into the ripped rhombi of sidewalks
—in clusters and scattered perspectives
of shining and torn misadventures.

Pedestrians, vehicles, trolleys
move and tremble in hundreds
and foreheads scaffold
the labyrinthine buildings.

Wide-opened blue windows
consume the floating spaces without.
Over the stair-rail, a dizzy view of the liminal—
—what a monumental stony creation.

You grow into clouds blindly:
straight, cold, and solid—
checkered buildings of the happy,
you stare into cloudy abysses.

The eyes of your mutable windows
will not reflect the dandelion's specter
that is winged in dove's flight
above the vast marble of white plains.

At dawn, in a white mist of morning
the worry won't flash through the cranny
that, somewhere in the ocean depths,
is a drowned moment of boyhood.

І росяна туга не склиться
за всім найдорожчим — пропалим,
— лиш меркнуть пов'ялені лиця
на шибах ослизлих підвалів.

Початі із креслень паперу,
підоймами рук перейняті,
воплотивши жорстоко — химеру
майстрів копітких і завзятих,

ви стали на грані уявлень
над хлюскотом хвиль океану —
мов дійсний, найдійсніший камінь,
що виріс в надхмарну оману.

Не брили, не звали клубовищ, —
— важенний крутіж переміни!
— І серця тремтіння не зловиш
у рокоті злім хуртовини!

Не зловиш, не стиснеш в долонях,
щоб серце замкнути од світу
і в оранжерійнім полоні
пустоцвітом трухло рясніти.

А серце — у трепоті крови
кружляє, мов глобус цвітучий,
по соняшних рейках невловних,
повз бурі, громи і повз тучі …

Плине течією у струменях,
Горить у машкарах пожарів,
— аж вмить, летючи, обезуміє
і світ свій ущент розударить —

і бевкне в бескеття і зойкне,
розколоте у безгомінні,
ненаситне, незаспокоєне
серце людини.

1949

And dew sadness doesn't luster
for the dearest and forgotten—
sad withered faces simply fade
in the windows of these sleazy basements.

You started as blueprints on paper,
permeated with handlevers,
gave birth to outrageous chimera
of painstaking audacious masters,

you stood between lines of impressions
above splashing waves in blue oceans—
like stone of an uttermost realness,
overgrown into aery delusion.

No bricks and no piles of billows
—a ponderous whirlpool of changes!
—Unable to catch how hearts tremble
in this vicious rumble of blizzards!

You won't catch it, won't grip for a moment,
to close your heart against the world
while captive in this greenhouse
You shine with putrid, barren flowers.

A heart whirls in bloody shivers
like a blooming globe
on sun-sparkling crossbars that could be seized,
to weather these storms, thunders, clouds . . .

It streams like a current,
Burns in a mask of fire
—abruptly flies, frantic and foolish,
to shatter its world—

and drums into aeons and shrieks,
splits inside this silence—
insatiable, anxious
is heart of a mortal.

1949

Translated by Olga Gerasymiv, Oleksandr Fraze-Frazenko, and Jazlyn Kraft

Гарлем

Ніч (I)

Із брам і ущелин хватають
чорним полум'ям рук. Загортають
в любашну і трепітну слизькість губ
і у випуклий вигиб задів.
І потім — очам, яких чорність бездонна
рудіє у відблисках гострих жаги,
дають матовість білих наложниць —
чорні дівчата Гарлему.

З таверн млосно клубиться сопух,
пересочений вишумом пива і сечі,
заялозений похіттю й потом
засмаглих і звинних тіл.

Знічев'я рябіє уривчасто — сміх,
що подібний до грудок консерви
із кінського м'яса.
Підскакують тупотом румби і мамбо
зелені світла ліхтарів
і темні бервена одвірків.

І раптом десь — крик,
що блиснув, мов ніж
у руці чорношкірій.
І мідяки задзвонили, мов сміх,
що скотився по сходах
до бурих відтулин каналу.

1957

Harlem

Night (I)

Out of gates and gorges they grab
with black flames of hands, wrapping
in lust and trembling the slickness of lips,
into the curved arcs of behinds.
And then—eyes, with bottomless blackness,
turning gingerly the reflections of acute thirst,
will be made pale white concubines—
black girls of Harlem

The stench balls languidly from taverns
soaked with the noise of beer and urine,
filthy with the lust and sweat
of those agile tanned bodies.

Carelessness speckles in jerks,
and laughter looks like canned lumps
of horse meat.
Jumping and stomping rumbas and mambos,
green colors of street lights,
and dark logs of the doors' jambs.

And suddenly, somewhere—a scream
shone like a knife
in a black skinned hand.
And copper coins rang like laughter
that rolled down the stairs
to the brown pits of the canal

1957

Інтермецо (II)

Але і є
ательє,
чорна магія
і цирк.
Вздовж і вшир —
з усіх архіпелагів є.
І тубільчий там-там,
з черепів тиміям,
голий скальп,
і сіямських сестер
конвульсійний вальс.
Усього подосталь:
ігор і жертв.

Є свої Мадонни,
і свої ікони,
свої нонни, свої бонни,
свої Мони
Лізи, —
і лакеї, і лакизи,
все своє,
і свій доктор Фавст.

І зусушений пуп —
бородань книгочій,
грошороб, женолюб
— люнатичні вночі.

Єрихонський зойк труб
у каналів намул!
Зброд — у твань!
            Перегул
— задушить, заглушить
чорним грюком машин,
гнівним громом душі,
яку зжер Вельзевул.

Intermezzo (II)

All is there
an atelier,
black magic
and circus
Length and breadth—
of all archipelagos is there.
And their barbaric drum,
smell of skulls,
naked scalp,
and the convulsive dance
of these Siamese twins.
More than enough of everything:
victims and games.

There are Madonnas,
and their own icons
own nonnas, own bonnas
own Mona
Lisas,
and lackeys, and butlers—
all of their own,
even one doctor Faust

There is a dry navel,
bearded scribe,
lover boy, moneymaker—
lunatics of the night.

Jericho cry of pipes
in silted canals!
Scum—in the dirt!
                    Echoing buzz
will strangle, will drown
with black rumble of cars,
angry thunder of souls
eaten by Beelzebub.

От і все. І кінець.
Чорна крапка. Ніщо.
Шкереберть —
ветхий жрець
таємниць:
білий чорт.

1957

That is all. The End.
Black full stop. Nothing more.
Upside down—
an old priest
of all mysteries

has a devil's white core.

1957

День (III)

Там бродять в білий день
від вулиці до вулиці —
порожні і зажурені,
волочать чорну іншість,
такі самі, як ми,
— роззяви і поети, і комедіянти,
і ті, що з тривогою
очікують важкого материнства.
Усі такі, як ми,
Але ще більш людські,
Ще правдивіші.
Їм сняться часом ще:
Канчук цукрової плянтації,
тропічна ніч і тесаний
в гебані — ідол,
що щастя їм дає.
Але це щастя десь за океаном,
на іншім суходолі, або й — ні …
— щастя — чорне, негритянське,
таке, як і вони самі.

1957

Day (III)

They roam in white day
from one street to the next,
empty and sad,
dragging black otherness,
the same kind as we—
gapers, poets, comedians,
and those who, in worry,
expect their burdensome motherhood.
The same kind as we,
but even more human,
even more truthful.
They dream some nights of
lashes on sugar plantations,
tropical night, an idol
hewn out of an ebony tree;
he brings joy.
That joy is somewhere overseas,
in other lands to linger elsewhere…
A black joy, Negro joy,

that joy so tightly their faces bare.

1957

Translated by Olga Gerasymiv and Jazlyn Kraft

Люди осілі

Вибубнюють і виплескують ідолів і табу.
Вигойдують бедрами кукли живих новородків.
І ночі бредуть, і дні — як обух,
важенні, кошлаті й короткі.

Їх маски, прогірклі горілкою і тютюном,
виблискують під мандоліною місяця мертво,
— і ніч обертається вибляклим дном
над вижертим попелом жертви.

Затьмарені очі спливають, хоч хтиво шукає рука
плодів, потонулих — каменем у безконечність,
— лиш кубляться тепло припливами молока
тіла повногрудих танечниць.

1960

Settlers

Drumming and clapping of idols and taboos.
Dolls of the living newborns are swinging hips.

And night crawls, and days are heavy, shaggy,
and short, like the butt of an axe.

Their masks soaked in vodka reek of tobacco,
sparkle deadly under the moon's mandolin
and the night becomes a pale bottom
over the ashes of victims eaten.

Tarnished eyes are afloat, but voluptuous arms
look for fruits drowned as stones into infinity,
—only the bodies of bosomy dancers
make warm nests in milky tides.

1960

Translated by Olga Gerasymiv and Jazlyn Kraft

Ніч на Іст-Бронксі

Корицевий запах, бананові грона,
горіхи, мигдалі — між смаглих облич,
і кучерява із глини Мадонна
з-за кіптяви диму вдивляється в ніч.

У скривленій брамі під оловом вікон,
де гори коробок, лушпиння й газет,
якийсь Дон Хуан, що прибув з Порто-Ріко,
масні теревені дівчатам верзе.

Рвучкі, наче сарни, засмагло вишневі,
ворушаться в танець, лиш вчують банґо, —
— крізь далеч проскиглюють втомлено меви,
і в'ється їх жаль, хоч не бачить ніхто.

У плямах жовтіють віддалені площі —
бліді острови, й відпливають ген-ген …
Лиш часом здається у відсвіті ночі,
що десь повз провулок метнувся Ґоґен,

в крилатій мантильї, високий і гордий,
із полум'ям шалу у корчах руки, —
закривши собою тривожні простори
ще не відкритих земель і віків.

1962

A Night in East Bronx

Banana bunches and cinnamon smells,
walnuts, almonds among dark-skinned faces,
and a curly Madonna made of clay
look into the night through sooty smoke.

Under the warped gate, under the window
lay stashes of boxes, newspapers, husks.
A new Don Juan came from Puerto Rico,
slick, chatting up the girls.

Dashing as chamois, tan as wild cherries,
starting dances to the sound of a banjo,
distantly, the seagulls wearily squawk,
though none see their sadness curling in awe.

Far off, the squares become yellow stained—
further, further pale islands sail away.
Sometimes it seems through a glow in the dark
that down the alley Gauguin dashes out.

He wears a winged mantle, tall and proud,
with flames of fury and cramping hands—
he closes with his body these troubling expanses
of yet undiscovered ages and lands.

1962

Translated by Olga Gerasymiv and Jazlyn Kraft

Юрій Косач

Мангаттен, 103-тя вулиця

тисячі рук — трепетних кобр
тисячі ніг на стежках до раю.

боже з жовтими очима
матінко на чорному ослику
їдучи в египет
по шляху де осипаються камінці
по трудному шляху збігців
знедолених і невольних
подайте чорного хліба
хліба якого не сіють
хліба якого не жнуть
хліба раю
з деревами де гойдаються
червонопері какаду
і солодкі яблука ростуть
первородного

дівчина — голубе торнадо
вухом її біси вповзають
щоб вповзти в живіт
і вертіти ним як одурілим
сонцем
зуби зуби зуби
цокотом перлистого граду
зуби зуби зуби
фіолетні риби
піймані в глибах місячних рель
наситять не одного
тисячі
чорних людей.

\<1958\>

66

Yuri Kosach

Manhattan, 103rd Street

thousands of arms like quivering cobras
thousands of legs on the footpaths to heaven.

o god with the yellow eyes
o mother on the black donkey
going to Egypt
down the path with the falling stones
down the difficult path of refugees
hapless and unfree
pass the black bread
the bread that isn't sown
the bread that isn't reaped
the bread of heaven
with the trees where the red-feathered
cockatoo rocks
and the sweet apples of original
sin grow

the girl is a blue tornado
demons crawl in through her ear
to crawl into her belly
and spin it like a crazed
sun
teeth teeth teeth
the chattering of pearly hail
teeth teeth teeth
violet fish
caught in the depths of lunar swings
sate not one
but thousands
of black people.

<1958>

Translated by Ali Kinsella

Нью-йоркська елегія

І кручі, і бескеття будівель,
І кліті риштів, зринулих в безодні,
Сирого неба — брили чорних скель,
Граніт каньйонів, пустирі безводні.

І рик племен, ув'язнених, мов звір,
В сліпих цямриннях, де згаса світання,
І зойк одчаю, чорний зойк зневір,
І смерть самотня, хижа на розстаю.

Ти все спізнав ущерть, ти все збагнув
У горні літ, у полум'ї відроджень.
Ти з криці викував троянду запашну:
Нема тут попелищ. Є тільки гнів і гордість.

<1966>

New York Elegy

Both the cliffs and the precipices of buildings
And the cages of scaffolding, cast into the abyss
The damp sky, boulders of black rock,
The granite of canyons, the waterless voids,

And the roar of tribes imprisoned like beasts
In the blind recesses where daylight dies
And the wail of despair, the black wail of the despondent
And lonely, predatory death on the shining path …

You completely understand, you figured it all out,
In the furnace of the years, in the flames of rebirth,
You have forged a fragrant rose from steel:
There are no ash heaps here! There is only wrath and pride.

<1966>

Translated by Ali Kinsella

Бродвей

Поплив він сурмами в столику ніч,
завив валторнами моторів, відвалив драпіжні брили,
щоб завулки, пащі бірж і темінь брам заголосили
по заграві, зів'ялій серед мли.
по заграві, умерлій на світанні.
І ніч відстукує хвилини куті
скляними гранями прозорих будівель,
і ніч, карбована прибоями юрби,
повзе удавом крізь асфальтів плити,
крізь джунглі камінюччя, звали скель,
щоб гад слизький, отрутою налитий,
світючим черевом життя живе давив.
О захисте ділка, банкіра і пронози,
о шелесте захланного банкнота,
о всеспустошуючий боже,
утверджений на кам'яних висотах,
в почеті кациків холодного Волл-стріту,
пливеш, пливеш, мов ідол мертвоокий,
безоднями безликого Бродвею,
і нишкнуть юрби, звірі, діти,
коли по здобич виповза удав,
й повзе по сходинках святого Вавилону,
розніжений веселками неону,
волочить тілища важкого звої
по мармуру гудючих капищ,
де витліває електронний робот,
рабу живому брат,
невільнику отому,
що поміж карбами нічної зміни,
зсутулений, осліплий і глухий,
народжений в закиненій щілині,
поміж залізям, сопухом жебрачих хиж,
свій вік без імені відробить,
щоб на міських дешевих цвинтарях
нікчемним брухтом догоріти.
Чи є ще джерело під цим асфальтом,

Broadway

Hailed by bugles it sailed into the multitudinous night
howled with the motors' French horns, it cast aside the rapacious boulders
so the alleys, the jaws of the markets
                              and darkness of passageways might shriek
after the flash that perished in the fog
after the flash that wilted at daybreak.
And the night beats out the minutes forged
by the glass facets of transparent buildings,
and o night, notched by the tides of the crowd,
crawl like a boa along the slabs of asphalt,
through the stony jungles; knock over the rocks,
so the slippery asp, filled with poison,
can crush the living life with its glowing belly.
O you defender of hustlers, bankers, and scoundrels,
o rustle of the covetous banknote,
o omniruinous God,
affixed upon the rocky heights
respected by the caciques on cold Wall Street,
you glide, glide like a dead-eyed idol,
along the abysses of faceless Broadway.
And the crowds, beasts, and children go silent
when the boa slinks toward its prey,
creeps along the steps of holy Babylon
softened by the neon rainbows,
drags its heavy, spiraled body
along the marble of the humming altars,
where the electric robot smolders,
brother to the living slave, to that captive,
who works namelessly his whole life
between the notches of the night shift,
slouched, blinded, and deaf,
born in a forgotten crevice,
among the iron, the stench of beggars' shanties,
so he may burn out like worthless junk
in the cheap, local cemetery.
Is there yet a spring beneath that asphalt,

чи є живі в пустелі без світань?
Чи під громаддями базальту
ще мерехтить осердя сподівань?
А може, гейзером ще видзвенить, спурхне
крицевокрила мрія, щоб в звитягах
мов урагану прапор, заспівати
і кармазином пропалати,
як заграв провісних наснага?

Каньйони вулиць вмаєш ще, Бродвей,
заб'ється серце не камінне, ще живе,
і, стрінувши людину, друже,
у час дзвінкий, коли асфальтом пророста
зеленошумне слово, слово дуже,
промовиш через хугу й дощ:
«Ні, не минайся,
            будь,
            повстань!»

<1966>

are there yet the living in the dawnless desert?
Does yet a nucleus of hopes twinkle
beneath the basalt behemoths?
Perhaps a steel-winged dream will yet take flight,
ring out like a geyser, so it may wave
in victory like the flag of the hurricane
and be consumed in a scarlet fire
like the zeal of prophetic flares?
You'll still have your canyons of streets, Broadway,
your still-stone, still-alive heart will beat,
and, having met someone, dear friend,
in the sonorous time, when the green-noise
word, the strong word, will be overgrown with asphalt,
you'll utter:

        don't pass on by,

                be,

                    rise up!

<1966>

Translated by Ali Kinsella

Авеню діамантів

Гасне прозолоть літа, індійського літа
у скляних саркофагах мовчазних споруд,
самота — як хмара — в оранжевім вітрі
висне маревом крил понад плесом отрут.

Між бескеттями, в урвищах давнього брану,
з попелищ Вавилона, з Ассирії надр
виростає потвора, і гул урагану
дудонить над пустелями зваги і зрад.

Ось за вильотом викресав скалками скелю
кінний велет, рабів ватажок — Болівар.
Йому б Анди бунтарські, та хитрий Рокфеллер
орлий обрій в сталеве ярмо закутав.

Височить авеню, розстилає безодні,
де калічить людину облуди іржа,
де сичать і палають пожежі неонів,
нависають над містом, як лезо ножа.

Крізь безлюддя асфальтів раби одержимі,
навіжені сновиди наосліп біжать,
де самумів одчай, де веселка крижини,
де дощі діамантів, де золота жар.

Ось дебелий боксер і вгодований гангстер,
кардинал і галайстра шляхетних падлюк
і прудкого «лінкольна» сіяючий панцир
пропливають повз нетрі фарбованих шлюх.

Їм чманіти, мов нетлям, б'ючись у вітрини,
за якими міниться мана золота,
витлівають медузами скорбні перлини,
і жемчужну жарінь хижа ніч огорта.

О ловці тих перлин із глибин океану,
трударі у проваллі алмазних тих шахт,
скільки треба ще сліз, щоб скипів полум'яно,
засвітився зорею отой діамант?..

Diamond District

The gilt of summer, Indian summer, goes out
in the glass sarcophagi of the silent structures
loneliness hangs like a cloud in the orange wind,
a mirage of wings above the pool of poison.

Between the precipices, in the gorges of ancient captivity,
from the ashes of Babylon, from the bowels of Assyria
grows a monster, and the howl of the hurricane
reverberates above the deserts of grit and betrayals.

Here around the corner, that giant of a man, Bolívar,
the leader of slaves, ignites splinters of rock.
His are the rebel Andes, but sly Rockefeller has
enfettered the eagle's freedom in a steel yoke.

The avenue leaps forth, spreads into the abyss,
where the rust of deceit cripples people,
where the neon fires hiss and burn,
hanging over the city like the blade of a knife.

The possessed slaves, the deranged dreamers
run blindly over the deserted asphalt
with the dust storms of despair, with the rainbow of ice,
with its rains of diamonds and golden ember.

Here the stout boxer and the well-fed gangster,
the cardinal and horde of noble scum
and the gleaming carapace of the swift Lincoln
glide through slums of painted harlots.

They go crazy beating like moths at the windows,
Behind which glimmers the manna of gold,
the woeful pearls smolder like medusas
and the predatory night enshrouds the nacreous heat.

O, divers for these pearls in the ocean depths,
o, laborers in the chasms of those diamond mines,
how many tears are still needed for this diamond
to boil in flames, to glow like a star? . . .

Авеню ще не лине у сонячні тали,
ще підвівся світанок, мов зморений кат,
крамарюючи кров'ю, статечні міняйли
сиплють жемчуг у гирла неситих гармат.

Так приходь же окраєм безлюдь, Дамаянті,
повз бескеття, що рветься шпилями до хмар.
Ти ж бо знаєш — свічіння оцих діамантів
люд штовхає у прірву, на смерть і на згар.

Ти — мій гнів, Дамаянті з чудесного краю,
це моя у твоїй полум'яна рука.
В наших грудях давно вже бурлить і палає
гніву твого й мойого невгасний вулкан.

<1966>

The avenue does not yet drift through the sun's rays,
dawn has not yet risen like a weary hangman;
contemplative moneychangers trading in blood
pour pearls into the mouths of insatiable cannon.

So come through that deserted land, Damayanti,
along the precipice whose spires thrust to the clouds.
You must know—the glow of these diamonds
pushes humanity into the abyss, to death and to the ashes.

Damayanti from the wondrous kingdom, you are my wrath,
this is my flaming hand in yours.
The unquenchable volcano of yours and my
wrath has long surged and burned in our breasts.

<1966>

Translated by Ali Kinsella

З пісень Гарлему

Громохкий міст, потвора велелюддя,
і сонце — колом багряним
вже подалось за Сто десяту,
щоб конха ночі спалахнула,
осяяла цямриння ям і нір,
асфальтів надра сколихнула,
камінним віттям загула,
вітрилами невольницьких трирем —
важких, брилястих,
як Гарлем.

Шумуй, у ніч ішовши, вий,
Сто двадцять п'ята,
Риком стугони підвалів чорних,
Де сопухів отруйна мла,
Де темінь, тлінь, де смерть —
Горбата плакальниця — домовину,
З дощок тендітних збиту, супроводить
І визволя людину із ярем.
Гарлем,
у слизі, у гнилизні,
в ядучій пастці жаг,
в тваринному скиглінні, у пітьмі, —
рабів одра, сліпих рабів тих натовп.

І їм гугнявий пастор прорікає
ім'я Христа, ім'я Христа
і відсвітом неонного хреста
благословить розстай
цих авеню, що линуть аж у рай,
цих авеню, що, сповнені рабами,
клекочуть, мов вулкан,
мов чорний ураган.

О ти, розп'ятий, не зійдеш,
щоб тричі нас, розп'ятих, потішати
підступливим, облудним словом.

From the Song of Harlem

The thunderous bridge, the monster of the multitudes
and the sun, that scarlet circle,
has already gone down on One Hundred Tenth
so the conch of night might flare up,
might illuminate the recesses of pits and dens,
stir up the asphalt entrails
whir like stone branches
like the sails of slave galleys
heavy and blocky
like Harlem.

Make noise, moving through the night, howl,
One Hundred Twenty-Fifth,
Roar for the black basements
With the poisonous haze of fetor,
With the darkness, cinders, where death
That humpbacked mourner, accompanies
The coffin nailed from fragile boards,
And liberates people from their yokes.
Harlem,
in slime, in rot,
in the caustic trap of desires,
in the animal whimper, in the darkness,
is a horde of slaves, that throng of blind slaves.

The nasally pastor preaches to them
the name of Christ, the name of Christ
and the reflection of the neon cross
blesses the path
of these avenues that soar up to heaven,
of these avenues that, full of slaves,
seethe like volcanoes,
like a black hurricane.

O you, crucified, you won't get down,
to delight us crucified ones a third time
with your cunning, deceitful word.

Замовкни, боже, у Гарлемі,
Бо царст не тих, що в небесах, він жде.
І день іде в безодню,
із чорних нір, з ядучих цих щілин,
з цямрин, де кімшаться, їх діти,
із брам, де сестри їх повіями стоять,
із мороку корчом, де блазнем став варнак,
із чаду, хмелю, злочину і злиднів
виходить він назустріч урагану,
виходить він — невольник і титан.

Шумуй, Сто двадцять п'ята,
в шори взята!
Камінні віти гнуться, спалахнув асфальт
І дудонить, і дудонить: «Ідемо!
Ідемо ми, ідем!»
Багряна ніч.
          На пагорбах —
                    Гарлем.

<1966>

Shut up, o lord, in Harlem,
It's not those kingdoms in heaven that he awaits.
And the day goes into the abyss,
from the black burrows, from the caustic crevices,
from the hiding places where their children play,
from the passages where their sisters whore,
from the gloom of pubs, where the convict's become the jester
from the noxious fumes, the rye, the crime and destitution
he comes out to meet the hurricane,
he comes out—a captive and titan.

Make noise, One Hundred Twenty-Fifth,
harnessed in chains!
The stone branches bow, the asphalt burns
And he rumbles and rumbles: "We're coming!
Coming, we're coming!"
Scarlet night.
        On the hills stands
                        Harlem.

<1966>

Translated by Ali Kinsella

Балада про Золотий Бродвей

Це пливе корабель, це фрегат Золотого Бродвея,
Тільки — скрізь там мерці, аж до самого дна,
Лиш скелети дзвенять, що повисли на реях.
І останнім іде, вже непевний своєї хотьби, капітан;
Утікає земля із-під ніг, наче устриця, зойкне і втихне
Душа золотого вина, і схопоне янтар.

Так признань ворохобних потахне жевріючий віхоть,
І нікому до того — зорі над завулком, мені,
Що на цьому фрегаті раюють повії, кати і опришки,
Серед спорзного скла, серед флейт, і клятьби, і вогнів
Веремія блаженних,
Приречених вишкір.

Гей, поете, мій брате, сновидо ось цих цвинтарищ,
Мій товаришу в мандрах, о Марло, о давній!
Обійняти б тебе, відшукавши в юрбі,
Серед люду мерзенного блазнів.
Де барився? Де ніч ночував, чародію?
Та не сердься, ти, либонь, з бездом'я прийшов,
Посідаємо вкупі, спитаю, а може, й не смію,
Тільки справді, наприклад, а чом

Аж у третьому акті ти вбив
Це знеможене серце поета?
Ось скажи — постривай, ми ж бо друзі собі.
Чи не краще утяти інакше?
А чому б не боротись та в цій боротьбі
Навіть впасти — не краще б?
Хай палає трагедій одвічний вогонь!
Хай життя, хай ненависть, хай крига!
Хай це кров, кров ненаситі серця твого!
Хай це подвиг, хай буря, хай вихор!
Позітни-бо свічіннями леза набряклий пістряк,
Що зсизів королю на пухкому його підборідді!
Вже пора, щоб у гроні лакиз і сутяг
Став суддею поет на покару огиді!

Ballad of Golden Broadway

This is the sailing ship, this is the frigate *Golden Broadway*,
It's just…the dead are everywhere, all the way to the bottom,
Only their skeletons hang jingling on the spars.
And the captain goes last, his step no longer sure;
The earth flees from underfoot, like an oyster, the golden wine's
soul wails and calms, and the amber grows cold.

Thus the smoldering straw of rebellious confessions will go out,
And no one will care, not the star above the alley, nor I,
That prostitutes, hangmen, and crooks on this frigate are in paradise
Among the dirty glass, among the flutes and the curse and the fires—
The uproar of the touched,
The grin of the doomed.

Hey, poet, brother mine, sleepwalker of these vast cemeteries,
My companion on the journey, o Marlowe, o ancient!
I'd embrace you, having found you in the crowd,
Among the jesters of the nasty people.
Where did you linger? Where did you spend the night, magician?
But don't get angry, perhaps you've known homelessness,
Let's sit together, I'll ask or maybe courage will fail me,
Only really, for example, but why

You waited to the third act to kill
That wearied heart of the poet?
Tell me this, wait a minute, we're friends after all.
Is it not better to do it another way?
Or why not fight that fight
Would it not be better, even if you fall?
Let the eternal fire of tragedies burn!
Let there be life, let there be hate, be ice!
Let it be blood, the blood of your insatiable heart!
Let it be a triumph, let there be a storm, a whirlwind!
With the flash of a blade, slice the swollen pimple
Rotting blue on the king's soft chin.
From among the lackeys and swindlers, it's time
For a poet to become judge and punish the ugliness!

«Проминай, ти — причинний!» — рече капітан.

Та й вона — синьовія Офелія з пустки неонів Бродвея.

Ні, пірате, ще мислить, живе моє «я», ще живе,

Не причинні — тверезі ми з Марло,

Коли хочеш, пливімо звідсіль в океан,

Тільки швидше, за обрій, за скарбами!

Є країна, що квіттям умаяна вічним,

Є країна, де радість триває,

Є країна, де посміхів щастя не лічать,

Є країна, де пісня одвіку лунає …

Гей, суворосте, в пастці примар!

(Це ж пливе корабель, це ж фрегат Золотого Бродвея).

Голубінь рвійнокрила свічіє з-за хмар!

(Лиш скелети дзвенять, що повисли на реях).

В муть тремку фіолетних заток,

У кришитальність невгавного скресу

Ринуть луни останні драпіжних оркестр,

І за мить корабель цей замовкне.

Ще свічіє Бродвей, що триває бенкет,

Але ми, хоч причинні, минімо,

Полишім цю галайстру піратів, проноз

(Хай їх реготу скрегіт імлою зависне!).

Нам-бо стелиться шлях у простори чудесні,

Швидше з крилами гроз!

Швидше з зорями в весни!

<1966>

"You shall pass, you are mad!" says the captain.
So is she, blue-lashed Ophelia from the neon desert of Broadway.
No, pirate, it still thinks, my "I" is alive, still alive,
Marlowe and I are sober, not mad
When you want, we'll sail from here into the ocean,
Only soon, beyond the horizon in search of treasures!
There is a country bedecked in everlasting flowers,
There is a country where happiness endures,
There is a country where smiles of joy can't be counted,
There is a country where the song sounds eternal…
Hey, austerity, in the trap of ghosts!
(This is the sailing ship, this is the frigate *Golden Broadway*.)
The restive-winged azure glows from behind the clouds!
(Only their skeletons hang jingling on the spars.)
In the quivering murkiness of violet gulfs,
In the crystal clarity of the unstoppable spring thaw
The last echoes of the rapacious orchestras surge.
And the ship will silence this in an instant.

Broadway still glows, the banquet continues
But, though we may be mad, let's pass it by,
Let's leave this horde of pirates, of scoundrels
(May the screeching of their laughter hang in a haze!).
We must pave the way to the wondrous places,
Faster on the wings of the tempests!
Faster with the stars in spring!

<1966>

Translated by Ali Kinsella

Андрій Малишко

Маяковський в Америці

За крутою хвилею, за океаном,
Задимлене сонце в хмарах тече,
Ходить він зі мною раннім-раном,
Положивши руку мені на плече.

По мосту, по бруклінськім, по Бродвею,
Біля хмарочосів кроком, як сталь,
Негритянську вулицю вгледить — і над нею
Теплими очима дивиться в даль.

В чорному Гарлемі діти негритята
Знають його посмішку й ласку руки,
Ходять біля нього і просять на свято
Докери, вантажники, робітники.

Він заводить з ними гарячу розмову,
Як би то їм правду вірніш знайти,
І разом знаходять правдиве слово,
І здається, — рідні вони брати.

І від того слова в нью-йоркському світі
Клевета і злоба кричать навспішки,
Хмуряться банкіри на Уолл-стріті,
З золотом ховаючи чорні мішки.

І свистить по вулицях вітер московський
Гнівом революцій видзвонює брук.
Здрастуй, мій учителю!
Здрастуй, Маяковський!
У мільйоннім потиску робітничих рук!

Там, за океаном, як вилита з криці,
Плеще твоя мова у братстві труда,
Кожне твоє слово родить у блискавиці,
Громом Батьківщини — твоя хода.

<1950>

Andriy Malyshko

Mayakovsky in America

Beyond tall waves, beyond the ocean,
Amidst clouds flows the smoky sun,
With me he walks in early morn,
And on my shoulder rests his arm.

Across Brooklyn's bridge, along Broadway,
Past skyscrapers our steps resound,
A Negro street meets his steely gaze,
While warm eyes peer above and beyond.

The Negro children in black Harlem
Know his smile and his hand's caress,
Dockers, loaders, workers walk with him,
And invite him to their labor fest.

With them he has a heated discourse
About how best the truth to find together,
And words of truth they find of course,
Indeed, it seems as if they're brothers.

These words provoke in New York's world
Quickened cries of slander and fury,
While hiding their black sacks of gold,
Wall Street bankers frown and worry.

The streets howl with Moscow's wind,
With revolution's rage sidewalks resound.
Greetings, my teacher!
Greetings, Mayakovsky!
To you worker millions their hands extend!

Beyond the ocean, as if molded from steel,
Your words resound amidst brothers of labor,
All you say has lightning's sharp feel,
While your walk is my Fatherland's thunder.

1950

Translated by Alexander Motyl

87

Леонід Лиман

Осінь у Бронкспарку

Як черепахи, десь повзуть віки,
І вітер шарпає уже останні квіти,
Поглянь, дитино, на оці листки,
Бо смерть землі відчують тільки діти.

Од вітру похитнулась довга тінь,
Здіймаються з-під землі камінні брили.
Це вже початок казки і марінь,
Якщо ми тут в осінній день ходили.

І лише хмари, вітер і піски —
Первісні відцвіли. Початку й насолоди,
А ці алеї, клюмби, таблички —
немов недоліки одвічної природи.

1951

Leonid Lyman

Autumn in a Bronx Park

The centuries crawl past like turtles,
The wind tugs on the last flowers,
Take a look, my child, at these leaves,
For only children feel the earth's death.

The wind has bent a long shadow,
boulders push up from under the soil.
This was the beginning of the fantasy and dreams
when we took a walk here on a fall day.

Only the primeval clouds, wind, and sand have
Bloomed away. Their beginning and delight,
And these alleys, flowerbeds and plaques are
like imperfections of nature eternal.

1951

Translated by Ostap Kin and Ali Kinsella

Юрій Тарнавський

Ода до кафе

О. Л. Вороневичу

I

о, тепле місце відпочивання тіла,

де можна розвісити мокрі полотна шкіри,

висушити на вітрі сухих, але ласкавих хвиль

піт втоми, ноги поставити, чекаючи

аж біль стече на долівку тихим скимлінням ножа,

за склом, в синьому світлі неба, боротимуться ще деякі:

на ґратах каналів лежатимуть мокрі, безголові трупи,

відходитимуть останки бунтівників

із без'язиким, німим прапором, але не розчаровані,

о, місце відпочивання сухих, як горіх, півкуль кучерявого мозку,

де можна, залишивши поле бою, оглядаючись,

перестати бути винним, дряпаним, ссаним всередині,

де можна майже заснути із ротом, повним смаку

молока жовтих грудей південних овочів,

де можна плакати приємними слізьми,

які течуть, як роса, із фіялкових очей,

де можна принести богові щастя

дві монети в жертву, заміняти за

дві хвилини лінивого спокою

о, святине немаючих святинь,

ти приймаєш в свої теплі долоні

сповідання залюблених і розчарованих,

слухаєш віршів поетів і крикливі розмови

філософів і мистців з чорними бородами,

ти пригортаєш їх до теплого, твердого живота,

прикриваючи великою долонею,

гладячи їхні спини і гладке волосся,

о, мати ридаючих сиріт,

ти віддаєшся бажаючим, як дешева повія,

продаєш біле, тепле тіло

молодим, що шукають наповнення,

і лишаєш їх спокійними і повільними, коли відійдуть

Yuriy Tarnawsky

Ode To A Café

To O. L. Voronevych

I

o warm place of rest for one's body,
where you can hang up the wet sheets of your skin,
dry off the sweat of fatigue in the wind
of dry but kind waves, stretch out your legs, waiting
for the pain to trickle down to the floor like the soft whimpering of a knife,
on the other side of the glass in the blue light of the sky some will still go on
    fighting:
on the gratings of sewers the wet headless corpses will lie undisturbed,
the rest of the rebels will retreat
with a mute, tongueless flag but not disappointed,
o place of rest for the dry walnut-like hemispheres of the curly-haired brain
where you can drowse with your mouth
full of the milk squeezed from the yellow breasts of tropical fruit,
where you can cry pleasant tears
which flow like dew from violet eyes,
where you can give two coins to the god of happiness
as an offering, in exchange for
two minutes of indolent peace

o temple of those who have no temples,
you accept into your warm hands
hopes of lovers and of the disappointed ones,
you listen to the poems of poets and to loud arguments
of philosophers and artists with black beards,
you press them to your hard, hot belly,
protecting them with your big hand,
stroking their backs and the lank hair,
o mother of orphans who keep on crying,
like a cheap whore you give yourselves to whoever wants you,
you sell your warm, white flesh
to the young ones who crave happiness
and you leave them silent and slow when they go away

II

в льодових ротах висить чорна ніч,
що смакує, як ніч тропіку,
що нагадує язикові
дихання, як в сполуці двох там-тамів

синім язиком співає цнотлива музика,
картини вже не снуються в черепі танцюючими,
лиш наростають тоді неясні хотіння
і знову цнотливо плаче теплою кров'ю серце

о, плач, кволе, боязливе серце:
я є усміхнено-задоволений болем,
плач, серце, в святині спокою,
де крізь сині вікна видно життя

1955–1956

II

in the icy mouths hangs a black night
which tastes like the night of the tropics
which makes the tongue remember
a breathing as in the coitus of two tom-toms

a prudish music sings with its blue tongue,
images no longer float dancer-like through your skull,
only vague desires now swell up inside you
and your heart cries once again its insipid warm tears of blood

cry my poor, timid heart,
I smile, relaxing happy in my pain,
cry my heart in this temple of peace
where life can be seen through blue windows

Ca. 1955–1956

Translated by the author

Неділі

I

серед в'язниці життя
неділі, як келії-одиночки,
пригадують про мури,
про самоту, жаль і кару,
про мрії, які втекли водою,
як неминучі години промов
повчальних, незносимих,
які приводять до божевілля
своєю впертою глупою настирливістю,
своїм безконечним джерелом падання
тяглими краплинами часу

II

в неділю життя пустіє від руху,
від машинального способу, який необдуманий,
від довгих тіней на роздоріжжях,
коли сходить і заходить сонце,
в неділю люди сплять,
сидять у м'яких кріслах, наслухаючись,
як останки бажання виходять
крізь пори дірявої шкіри
нудним запахом кадил,
наркотичними нитками диму,
в неділю серця холонуть:
вбирають у себе холод
голубих небесних тарелів,
стін кімнат і облич рідних,
і всередині видніє правда,
забута серед речей буття,
як дорогий камінь, сіяючий серед шмат,
як дорогий камінь, твердий і холодний,
в неділю гаснуть надії
і чорнилом наповнюються
рідким, терпким, чорним
думки людей

Sundays

I

in the prison house of life
Sundays are like solitary cells,
reminding one of walls,
of loneliness, guilt, and punishment,
of dreams that have flowed away like water,
they are like unavoidable sermons that last for hours,
teaching you what you should do, unbearable,
driving you to madness
with their stubborn, mindless insistence
their inexhaustible source of the dripping
of the viscous drops of time

II

on Sundays life grows empty of motion
of the mechanical way in which the brain plays no part,
of the long shadows at road crossings
when the sun rises and sets,
on Sundays people sleep,
relax in soft chairs,
watching the rest of their hopes escape
through the pores of their skin full of holes
like the sickening smell of incense,
like narcotic threads of smoke,
on Sundays people's hearts grow cold:
they absorb the chill of the blue celestial platters,
of the walls of the rooms and of the faces of their loved ones,
and inside suddenly shines the truth
forgotten among the things of existence
like a precious stone glittering among rags,
like a precious stone, hard and cold,
on Sundays people's hopes grow dim
and a black, caustic ink
fills their thoughts

III

в неділю наповняються кінотеатри
чорним волоссям людських голів,
теплою темрявою поту,
зіпсутим повітрям, від якого болить голова,
в театрах живуть актори
іменами й тілами інших,
скрипалі плачуть скрипками,
в бібліотеках книжки
наставляють під порох тіла,
гріючись до тихих вікон

IV

о, прийдуть після пісків століть
свіжі, як помаранчі, дні,
і потечуть у небо
водоспади вогняних морів:
які кипітимуть, розіллються і покриють
чорні долівки небес
рожевою рідиною,
і гладкою стане поверхня,
де були гори, ріки, міста,
і виростуть вітряні, просторі оселі
нових здорових людей,
з дорогим каменем правди,
гострим, твердим, ясним,
сіяючим в серці

1955–1956

III

on Sundays movie houses fill up
with the black hair on people's heads,
the warm darkness of sweat,
stale air that gives you a headache,
actors inside theaters live
with the bodies and names of others,
violinists cry with their violins,
inside libraries books
expose their bodies to dust
warming themselves against the quiet windows

IV

o but there will come after the sands of centuries
fresh, orange-like days,
and waterfalls of fire will roar up into the sky
boiling, spreading, and covering
the black floors of heavens
with a rose-colored liquid,
and the surface will turn smooth
where once there were mountains, rivers, and cities,
and spacious airy dwellings will spring up all around
belonging to new healthy people,
with the precious stone of truth,
sharp, hard, and shining,
glittering in their hearts

Ca. 1955–1956

Translated by the author

Любовний вірш

На це немає слів:
може, справді
ми закінчили нелегку школу любови.
Ти пам'ятаєш квадратові
неділі, придавлені кубами міста.

Пам'ятаєш, як дощ
покривав фосфором дороги
і як у високих пляшках вулиць
осідав чорний намул дня?

Усе пройшло.
Скажи, де ділися стогони
в гарячих легенях готелю?
Там тепер хтось розпинає повії
на білих ґолґотах ліжок.

<1959>

Love Poem

There are no words for it—
maybe it's true that we have finished
the difficult school of love.
You remember the square
Sundays under the heavy
cubes of the city.

Remember how rain
coated the roads with phosphorus
and how the black silt of evenings
settled in the tall bottles of the streets?

All is gone!

Tell me what happened to the moans
in the hot lungs of the hotel?

Now whores are being crucified here
on the white Golgothas of beds.

<1959>

Translated by the author

Приїзд IV

До подвійного перебування, що тривало по два тижні, на острові, форму якого перебрала моя душа; до кімнат, в яких неможливе поняття вікон; до мого мозку й язика у формі мурашників, що кишать від цифр; до машин, теж м'яких, немов із глини, і конусоїдних, в яких розводяться мурашки та сеча; до зору, що не міститься; до людей, з яких видимі лиш язики, чи олівці, чи крейда; до цигарок, частково заслонених мозками; до сходів з мови, під якими стогнуть людські душі; до перерв для зору; до ротів, що самі літають вулицями в шуканні їжі; до ресторанів, для темряви яких скуповують простір ротів; до моєї ходи за допомогою рота; до крамниць, від яких я обертаюся догори ногами і які стають частиною моєї уявної голови; до статевої приємности, перетвореної в папір; до сперматозоїдів і жіночих яєць, чорних і схожих на друк; до сірої та сухої менструальної крови на тротуарах, повної бациль туберкульози; до людей з розмішеними обличчями й душами, і з обличчями в черевах, і з ротами на колінах; до будинків, що рухаються й виглядають, як люди; до натовпів, що виглядають, як нещасливі грубі обличчя; до повісом слизі та жовтої сажі в повітрі; до диму з жовчі; до мого тіла, розтягненого від швидкости, як дим, зі смаком ґуми в ногах; до рогу вулиці, де за невелику ціну обтинають голови; до південного кінця острова з лез; до зарізаних людей, що блукають там, шукаючи своєї крови, зниклої за повітрям; до моря, що переходить у повітря; до сендвічів з лавок, і з металевих кошів, і з пальт, і з власних рук; до лавок, яких не можна відрізнити від підлітків, що граються, і від закоханих пар; до підлітків, що ховаються за далековидом і кімнатами, які далекі від них, щоб побачити мою душу; до мене, коли я стою побіч себе і бачу, як я ховаюся за своїм жуванням, що має форму безлистого куща, і за травленням мого шлунка у вигляді торби з брунатного паперу, і, дивлячися в сіль та в м'ясо, стараюся побачити Еспанію.

<1969>

Arrival IV

To a double stay, each lasting two weeks, on an island, whose shape my soul took on; to rooms, in which the concept of windows is impossible; to my brain and tongue in the shape of anthills teaming with numbers; to machines, also soft, as if made out of clay, and cone-shaped, full of ants and urine; to eyesight which is too big to fit in; to people, the only visible parts of whom are tongues, or pencils, or chalk; to cigarettes partly hidden behind minds; to staircases of speech under which moan people's souls; to recesses for one's eyesight; to mouths which fly alone through streets looking for food; to restaurants for the darkness inside of which they buy up the spaces of mouths; to my walk with the help of my mouth; to stores from which I turn upside down and which become part of my imaginary head; to sexual pleasure turned into paper; to sperms and women's eggs, black and looking like print; to gray and dry menstrual blood on the sidewalks full of the germs of TB; to people with their faces and souls kneaded like dough and with their faces in their bellies and with their mouths on their knees; to buildings which move and look like people; to crowds which look like fat unhappy faces; to skeins of mucus and yellow soot in the air; to the smoke of bile; to my body stretched out from speed like smoke with a taste of rubber in my feet; to the street corner where they chop off your head for a reasonable price; to the southern tip of the island made out of knife blades; to people with their throats slashed who wander around there looking for their blood which has vanished behind the air; to a sea which gradually becomes air; to sandwiches made out of park benches, and wire baskets, and overcoats, and one's own hands; to park benches you can't distinguish from teenagers who play games and from pairs of lovers; to teenagers who hide behind telescopes and rooms which are far from them, so as to see my soul; to me, as I stand next to myself and see myself hiding behind my own chewing in the form of a leaf-less bush, and behind my stomach digesting my food in the shape of a brown paper bag, and, looking into salt and meat, try to see Spain.

<1969>

Translated by the author

Кінець світу

Переїхав
міст,
без зусилля,
не плативши
за проїзд,
як кров,
випливаючи
з жили,
авто
котиться
по бетоні,
немов крізь
простір,
інші авта, грузовики,
котяться
повз мене,
яких
сто метрів
попереду,
де починається
пітьма,
напис
червоними, синіми й білими
літерами
на зеленім
тлі
сповіщає:
INTERSTATE
80 WEST
RT 17 NEWARK
EXIT
1/2 MILE.

<1978>

End of The World

Have driven
across the bridge
effortlessly,
without having to pay
the toll,
like blood
coming
out of vein,
the car
tumbles along
the concrete
as if through space,
other cars, trucks
tumble past me,
some hundred
yards ahead
where the darkness
starts
a sign
in red, blue, and white
on a green
background
proclaims:
INTERSTATE
80 WEST
RT 17 NEWARK
EXIT
1/2 MILE.

<1978>

Translated by the author

Сссмерть

Сухоребра
шкапа негоди
ледве волочить ноги вулицею,
дощ плеще
плітки про літо,
мозок в одну мить формолює
теорію дрожів,
майже Великдень,
скількісь там років тому,
такий собі молодець,
не дуже-то молодий,
під сороківку,
зі смолоскипами очей
і решток волосся,
ганяв крізь вісім-мільйонове місто
за маревами межиніжжя,
одна теж собі така
анорексійна панночка,
тхнуло їй з уст лятриною,
бо від учора
ні рисочки в роті,
щоб бути ще більше,
як Твиґґі,
водив її в руссский
ресссторан
їсти український борщ
і сссирну
руссску пасссску,
потім на концерт
ссстрастей
за СССв. Іваном Златоустттом,
у Карнеґі Голл,
під шкірою сссмерть
трясссеться (трусссится), як кролик,

Dddeath

The skin and bones
nag of bad weather
barely drags itself
down the street,
the rain
whispers bad things
about the summer,
the mind in one instant
formulates a theory of shivering,
almost Easter,
some X number or so years ago,
a certain young man,
not so young in reality,
pushing forty,
with the torches of his eyes blazing,
ran madly through an eight-million inhabitants city
in search of the mirages of crotches,
another certain similar one
anorexic young lady,
her breath smelling like a latrine
because she didn't have anything to eat
since the day before
in order to be still more
like Twiggy,
took her to a Russsian
ressstaurant
to eat Ukrainian borshch
and Russsian Eassster
cheese cake,
after that to a concert
in Carnegie Hall
to hear the Ssst. John Passsion,
under the skin dddeath
shakesss (shiversss) like a ssscared rabbit,

коли тримати за сссідниці,
аж ссстрашно,
ніби сссам граєш
сссвою-таки
сссмерть!

17.IV.1987

giving you the shiversss
as if you were fffucking
your own
fffucking dddeath.

April 17, 1987

Translated by the author

Богдан Рубчак

Бездомний

Обличчя — безструнна скрипка, запорошена і порожня.
Місто моментів — йому нудна, безбарвна вічність.
В очах — вулиця, що ніколи, ніколи не спинить;
Вчора, Завтра, Сьогодні блимають незмінними неонами.

Обличчя — прекрасна скульптура в дереві дорогому,
Стара скульптура, що закинена десь у підвалини;
А в душі, Боже! в душі Єремія ридає,
Сидячи на відламках трагічних, на руїнах будівель гордих.

Ні! Пестра вулиця ніколи нічим не спинить.
Пестра птиця, вогняна, часом у снах літає,
І не знати (ніби хтось голову взяв у долоні і тисне!) не знати,
Чи вона ласкава, чи очі видерти хоче.

Уста не говорять. Тільки брукові кажуть про смуток,
Тільки часом старечій стіні, немов мамі, розхлюпують болі.
Останній раз усміхнулись, коли він узяв ніжно в руки
Брудного голуба з роздертим крилом і пестив.

Голуб біле зболіле крило розпростер на чорний палець,
Собака-приблуда побиту голову тер об його втомлену ногу,
А обиватель, в якого душа, як крамничка, де продають рибу,
Його обминав, тремтячи за свій ситий портфель.

Уста усміхнулися … Потім, може, гарячкою зранені мрії
Прийшли — не про хатку, городчик, пошану сусідів —
А мрії про чисті гори, на яких сніги життєдайні,
Мрії про беріг, про дужі прибої, про шуми безмежжя …

I.1956

Bohdan Rubchak

Homeless

The face is a stringless violin, covered with dust and empty.
This city of moments—he's bored by colorless being.
In his eyes there is a street that will never slow him down;
Yesterday, Today, Tomorrow blink with the constancy of neon signs.

A face is a beautiful sculpture in a setting so rich,
An old sculpture cast off, lost in a basement;
And in his soul, oh Lord! In his soul Jeremiah cries,
Sitting on fragments so tragic, on the ruins of buildings once proud.

No! This motley street will slow for nothing.
This variegated bird, this firebird, careens into a dream
And it's not known (as if his head were taken into palms and squeezed!), not
     known—
whether the bird's gentle or wants to rip out his eyes.

Lips do not speak. Only to this stone road of sorrows
Only to this senile wall, motherly wall, they splash the pain.
Last time they smiled, he had gently taken in his hands
A dirty dove with a torn wing and caressed it.

The dove spread a white damaged wing over black fingers,
A stray dog rubbed its beaten head against his tired leg,

A man with a soul like a fishmonger's shop
passed him by, trembling for his fat briefcase.

The lips smiled… Then, maybe, dreams came—stricken with fever:
They are not of a house, or a garden, or respect from the neighbors—
But dreams of pure hills, with life-giving snows,
Dreams of the coast, of hefty waves, of immensity's noises.

January 1956

Translated by Olga Gerasymiv and Jazlyn Kraft

Богдан Бойчук

Вірші про місто

1

Я іду зустрітися,
Та місто
Затягнулося каменем,
Не йде
Мені напроти.

2

Я чекаю, поки
Стопляться під місяцем
Дахи
На Bleecker Street
І пам'ять набубнявіє
Від мітів.

3

Я іду зустрітися
З людьми
І прикладаю пальці
Їм до губ,
Але кривавлять
З дотику уста,
І я лишаюсь сам.

4

Мури
Тиснуть тих,
Які кохаються
Вночі,
Розшарпані
Гарячим саксофоном;

По коханні
Хлопець кидає в горнятко серця
Тридцять срібняків,
На дівчину лягає тінь.

Bohdan Boychuk

City Verses

1.
I'm going to a meeting
The city
Laced up in stone
Does not go
Against me

2.
I'm waiting for
The roofs
To melt under the moon
On Bleecker Street
And for memory to swell
From myths

3.
I'm going to meet
people
And lay my fingers
On their lips
But their mouths bleed
From the touch
And I remain alone

4.
Walls
Squeeze the ones
Who make love
At night,
Torn up
By a hot saxophone;

After sex
The boy tosses into the cup of his heart
Thirty pieces of silver,
A shadow lies down on the girl.

5

Більма вікон
Ломлять темряву,
В якій горять
Свічки жадання,
Біля витертих облич
На ложах.

6

Любовники
Закутуються
В теплі стіни.

Між ногами стогне
Зламана невинність,
Мов дорога в старість.

<1963, 1983>

5.

Cataracts of windows
Break the dark,
Where burn
The candles of desire,
Around the washed-out faces
On the couches.

6.

Lovers
Wrap themselves
In warm walls.

Between legs groans
Broken innocence,
Like the road to old age.

<1963, 1983>

Translated by Anand Dibble

Листи

Нью-Йорк, 11 вересня

Ми не знайомі, бо тебе ніхто ще іменем не сквернив. Ми зустрілися на водах ночі — ти прийшла м'якою стежкою сновиду. Води затремтіли й відійшли, немов відплив, у темряву. І я тебе не знаю, бо тебе ніхто ще іменем не сквернив, дівчино. Ти чиста. Бо ім'я — це пляма, на якій розмазано багато значень. Я радію, що тебе не знаю.

Гартфорд, 1 січня

Мене виштовхують години, а я не хочу йти, бо лячно. Години пхають і виштовхують за двері року, а я не хочу йти, хапаюся за спомини і думаю про тебе. Лячно, лячно йти у невідоме. Нам тепліший спомин, ніж життя, що мов чужа людина на дорозі. Мене лякає те, що невідоме. Нам Творець не дав частини свого серця.

Вашінґтон, 11 березня

Мені пора нагадує тебе: зелені пуп'янки підносяться з-під чорної сорочки і тривожать запахом весни. Брякнуть соками рослини, тужать проростанням — на одну весну, єдине літо! О, який короткий час. А моя весна — це спомин. Моя весна — це ти. А може, краще бути спомином, бо ми не вміємо прощати, як краса жінок стирається літами.

Сарасота, 1 серпня

Спека. Надмір сонця кривдить і висушує. Кусаючи плоди, калічимо уста смаком терпкої смерти, пахне пізньою любов'ю. Ми ніколи не знайомились устами. Мені чужі пісні твоїх колін. Чи дійсно, випивши кохану жінку, губимо найкращі почуття? Я не знаю, я ніколи уст твоїх не кривдив, нам не знаний запах пізньої любови, ані першої.

Нью-Йорк, 11 вересня

Я шукав тебе на вулицях Нью-Йорка. Та дарма, дарма. Вулиці душилися обличчями і пухли: втомою, нудьгою, перестоялим коханням, шмінкою роздертими устами. Час розмазував обличчя зморшками і потом, — гнав людей все ближче до кінця, ближче до кінця одної вулиці. Тебе там не було. Час не може розкладати старістю уяву. Ти не зміниш ніколи. Будеш молода.

Letters

New York, Sept. 11

We're strangers because no one defiled you with a name. We met one the night's black water, you came over the soft path of a dream. Water trembled and receded like a tide. And I don't know you, because nobody defiled you with a name. You are pure. For a name is a stain, blurred with many meanings. I'm glad I do not know you.

Hartford, Jan. 1

The hours elbow me, but I don't want to go. It's frightening. The hours push and shove me out the old year, but I refuse to go, hold on to my memories and think of you. It's frightening to step into the unknown. Remembrance is closer to us than life, which stands like a stranger on the road. I'm scared by the unknown. The Creator did not give us a shred of His heart.

Washington, March 11

The season reminds me of you: green buds rise through the black shirt and disturb with the smells of spring. Vegetation swells with sap, yearns to grow— for just one spring, one summer! Oh, what a narrow time! But my spring is only a memory. My spring is you. Maybe it is better that you remain a memory, because we don't know how to forgive when a woman's beauty wears down with age.

Sarasota, Aug. 1

Heat. Excess of sun wrongs and scorches. Biting fruits, we infect our mouths with a taste of death; smells of late love. I never bit your mouth. The songs of your hips are also unknown to me. After having drunk a loved woman, do we really lose our deepest feelings for her? I don't know. I never wronged your lips, we never knew the smell of late love.

New York, Sept. 11

I was looking for you on the streets of New York. A hopeless search. The streets choked with faces, swollen with weariness, boredom, stale loves. Time smeared the faces with sweat and wrinkles, drove them closer to the end of the last street. You were not there. Time cannot mark a dream by age. You will never change. You will be young.

Небо замовкає для людини. Крик позначених Творцем плянет нічого не говорить. Розтягаємо дороги на хитких драглистих ночах, і дороги нищать нас. Губимо сліди і тужно робиться за дотиком (чи має значення?) твоєї білої руки, за красою чорнобрового (чи має?) погляду, за прониканням молодого тіла, і тоді нам треба знати, як забути. Як усе забути.

<1963, 1983>

....

Heaven is dumb to creatures. The shouts of planets, marked by God, say nothing. We stretch out roads over gelatinous space and they strangle us. We lose our footprints and grieve for a touch (does it matter?) of your white hand, for the beauty (does it?) of a dark-eyed (does it?) glance, for the penetration of a girl's body. Then we have to learn how to forget. Everything.

<1963, 1983>

Translated by Mark Rudman in collaboration with the author

Негр сидить посередині дороги і б'є у барабан

З барабаном і чорним лицем
сів хлопчина, розкинувши ноги, —
над камінним надбитим плечем
зашморгнулись вузлами дороги.
Під асфальтовим потом пече
чорна шкіра шляхів і ятріє.
Барабанить хлопчина, і жаль
прилипає на вії;
з барабаном і болем в очах
місить пальцями звуки гугняві, —
на минулого білих полях
будить спомин смаглявий.
З барабаном. До нього пропах
подих предків з могили,
їхні кості скликає на суд,
щоб на бубнах ломились.
Щоб їх джезом пекло в черепи
і палило їм щоки,
щоб ставали з живими в ряди:
білозубі губаті пророки.

IX.1963

A Negro Sits in the Middle of the Road and Beats a Drum

With a drum and a black face
the boy sits, legs spread—,
above his stony cracked shoulder
the roads knotted tight.
Under the asphalt sweat the black skin
of paths bakes and glistens.
The boy drums with pity
stuck to his eyelids
with a drum and pain in his eyes
he produces the nasal sounds with his fingers—,
on the white fields of the past
he wakes a dark-skinned recollection.
With a drum. The breath
of ancestors has reached him from their grave,
their bones call to judgment,
to break apart on tambourines.
To have jazz burn in their skulls
and scorch their cheeks,
to line up with the living:
white-toothed, thick-lipped seers.

September 1963

Translated by Anand Dibble

Любов у трьох часах

Три

1

Помариш ще білолистям,
щоб виросло білими персами,
дівочі бедра облистило,
щоби обпестити;

помариш лопушим листям,
щоб стегна зеленим розплавило,
а потім плоскими долонями
щоб обласкавило.

2

ти мариш про білі стіни
що
мов чисті сторінки паперу
приймають тебе і синьооку дівчину

натомість
зашморгуєшся
в довгих вулицях

облипаєш
залицяннями мужчин на 42-гій вулиці
голими грудьми
ховзькими бедрами
набряклими устами

аж тебе опівночі розплощують
на зужитім тілі жінки
між брудними матерацами
обвислі стіни

наче божі руки

3

Я завжди марив її тілом. А тепер: дівчина стояла гола, входила у Стрипу. Прозорі ноги на білім камені, рвучка вода і біла дівчина — були, щоб їх приймати і любити. Дівчина залазила повільно в річку, її ноги то

From *Three Dimensional Love*

Three

1

You will dream that birch-white leaves
will cup her whitening breasts,
wrap around her hips and caress
her legs;

you'll dream of burdock leaves,
their sap pressing against her things,
lifting her toward you
on flat green hands.

2

you dream of whitewashed walls
that like empty pages
would accept you
and your blue-eyed girl

but you're strangled
by longs streets
propositioned by men
on 42nd St

plastered by
naked breasts
sweating hips
swollen lips

until the walls
flatten you at midnight
on the used woman's body
and a dirty mattress
like God's palms

3

I always dreamt of her body. Now she was naked, entering the river. Delicate legs over white stones and a freckled girl. Slowly she waded into the river, assuming strange shapes under the currents. She went deeper and deeper, until

видовжувалися, то дивно вигиналися під хвилями. Вона пірнала глибше, двома руками обнімала сонце і, дивно усміхаючись, плила до мене.

На Колійовій вулиці порожні стіни, мов незаписані сторінки паперу, мов немилосердні божі руки, тиснули мене ночами. У мурах корчилися постаті людей, випихали худі обличчя і кричали в темряву.

she embraced the sun with both hands and, with a hazy smile, swam toward me.

In my room on Railroad Street, the empty walls, like blank pages, like God's merciless hands, weighed down on me each night. Human shadows twisted inside those walls, pushed out their emaciated faces and shouted into the dark.

Одинадцять

1

Напне на грудях перкаль ночі,
обпарить губи кропом сосок;
знепритомнівши, неспокоєм
закропиш очі.

Зануриш голову у білу
Гущавину грудей кипучих,
Бажаючи ще раз вернутись
В жіноче тіло.

2

роздерши на грудях перкаль
вона переходить times square
і віддається кожному
хто прагне кохання
за гроші

і ти
самотній
також злягаєшся з нею
бо не маєш нікого
ближчого

3

Коли ми нарешті вибігли на гору, дівчина тяжко дихала, а присмерк прикривав її соски. Одягнувшись, ми стояли поруч і слухали, як внизу шуміла Стрипа, як над кручею німіли зорі. Ми були самі й щасливі. Але святі, які хапалися за побляклі рештки своєї вічності на мурах, випихали з-між каміння строгі лиця і не раділи з нами.

Після нічної акції на жидів, коли ґестапо ганяло порожніми кварталами, доловлюючи і дострілюючи, я ішов униз Колійовою вулицею до торговельної школи, яка стояла навпроти ратуші по другому боці Стрипи й одним плечем підтримувала горбок із старим кладовищем. Біля криниці Соб'єського я побачив жінку, яка лежала посеред вулиці, розкинувши руки. Її голова була розірвана пострілом, а з чашки тягнулася застигла кров і клапті липкого волосся. Збоку лежала відкрита торбинка, з якої сипались шпильки, коралі, гребінець…

1974–1976

Eleven

1

She'll shed the night's percale,
burn your lips with her breasts,
infect your moistened eyes
with unrest,

you'll dip your anxious brow,
in the white foam of her flesh,
turning to return
into her.

2

tearing apart her cotton dress
she crosses Times Square
and giver herself to everyone
who hungers for flesh
and pays

you
also make love to her
having no one
closer

3

In the monastery, dusk covered her nipples. Dressed, we stood next to each other and listened to the Strypa below, to the stars over the precipice. We were alone and happy. But the saints, who kept holding on to their faded eternity on the ruins, pushed out their fierce faces through the walls and did not rejoice with us.

After the night action on the Jews, as the Gestapo chased over the empty streets, hunting and shooting. I was headed down Railroad Street to the Commercial School. Near Sobiesky Well I saw a woman fallen in the middle of the street with her arms spread. Her head had been splintered by a bullet. Her hair was dark brown. At her side lay and opened handbag, spilling pins, beads, combs…

1974–1976
Translated by Mark Rudman in collaboration with the author

Ланчонетний триптих

Приїхавши до Америки,
я працював посудомийником

1

На непотребі нью-йоркського «давнтавну»
все було захоплююче того року:
блимаючі виклики неонів,
переяскравлені уста жінок,
пожмакана вата білого хліба,
якого я ніколи не мав вдосталь,
і навіть ланчонет на Верік вулиці,
де сотні тарілок, чашок і склянок
були приятелі моїм рукам.

2

Я працював лише два місяці
в тій забігайлівці
і вперше за десятиліття наситився,
Всі мене приймали мирно:
тарілки, які тримались долонь,
не падали,
власники-брати, гебрейської лагідности,
худенька італійка,
яка тоншала під кожним поглядом,
і широкозада Джоузі,
що розбовтувала і тривожила грудьми
густе повітря
і мій спокій.

3

Я працював лише два місяці,
та цілих двадцять літ
мене тривожили примари
ланчонетних снів.
Аж одного дня
я не витримав,
погнав до того ланчонету.

Luncheonette Triptych

Coming to America,
I worked as a dishwasher

1

In the trash of New York's downtown
everything was exciting that year:
the shimmering neon cries,
women's garish mouths,
the crumpled cotton of white bread,
the kind I never got enough of,
and even the luncheonette on Varick street,
where hundreds of plates, cups, and glasses
were buddies to my hands.

2

I worked only two months
in that joint
and for the first time in ten years got enough to eat,
They all accepted me peacefully:
the plates that held onto my palms,
didn't fall,
the owners—brothers with their Jewish tenderness,
the skinny Italian girl,
that got thinner under every glance,
and wide-hipped Josie,
that shook up and disturbed with her breasts
the thick air
and my calm.

3

I worked only two months,
yet for twenty whole years
I was disturbed by ghosts
of luncheonette dreams.
But one day
I couldn't resist,
ran off to that luncheonette.

Коли зайшов —
на мене вдарила
вільготна чужість:
все переінакшилось за ті роки,
стало незнайоме —
люди, двері, стіни, навіть посуд.

В ту хвилину часточка мого життя
неначе розчинилася в пливкій реальності,
поблякла.

І не сниться більше.

Відтоді я почуваюсь,
наче мені вирвано кусок минулого.

14.XII.1977, 1983

When I went in—
I got hit
with a humid oddness:
everything was altered in those years,
became unfamiliar—
people, doors, walls, even the dishes.

That minute it was as if a bit of my life
dissolved in wavering reality,
withered.

Now I don't dream about it.

From then on I felt
like a piece of my past was torn out.

December 14, 1977, 1983

Translated by Anand Dibble

Нью-Йоркська елегія

Нью-Йорк ковтає нас великими куснями,
перетравлює
і проганяє понурими венами
до остовпіння.

Задихнувшись переляком,
хапаємось

за розхилитані
двері,

за відчай
ослизлених тіл,

за краєць порожнечі —

аж камінь осідом вникає в жили
і сповільняє
порух клітин.

17.I.1978

New York Elegy

New York swallows us in big pieces,
digests
and drives us around gloomy veins
to stupor.

Breathless with fright,
we catch

at swinging
doors,

at the despair
of clammy bodies,

at a speck of void—

till the stone penetrates our veins like a precipitate
and slows
the movement of our cells.

January 17, 1978

Translated by Anand Dibble

Діма

Вечірній Бродвей

Реклями, реклями, реклями …
Над нами, з боків, під нами …
Реклями на кожному кроці,
Аж заболіло в оці.
Зелені,
Червоні,
Жовті,
Блискучі,
Бліді,
Барвисті
Реклями танцюють,
Реклями співають,
Реклями — вулькани неначе —
Вогонь та дим випускають …
Ідеш по Бродвею
У вечірню годину
І моторошно стає
Від отих кольорових плям …
І як тільки може людина
Витримать стільки реклям?

<1963>

Dima

Broadway in the Evening

Ads, ads, ads…
Above us, below us, on all sides…
Ads on every corner,
So many your eyes hurt.
Green
Red
Yellow
Bright
Pale
Colorful
Ads dance,
Ads sing,
Ads are like volcanoes
Putting off fire and smoke.
You walk along Broadway
In the evening
And it starts to feel creepy
From all those colorful stains…
How can a human being
Stand so many ads?

<1963>

Translated by Ostap Kin and Ali Kinsella

Нью-йоркська ніч

Ніч перерізано, розчахнуто навпіл
моторів ревом, виттям сирени,
нью-йоркських авт
рухом шаленим
і димом будинку,
що поруч горів.
Ніч закінчилась,
не почавши снів.

У вікна билося виття сирени
і знову марилось зелене
та тихе поле,
а над ним —
небесне чудо незабутнє —
малого жайворона спів.

<1984>

New York Night

The night is sliced, split into half
by the roar of engines, the wail of sirens,
by the mad traffic of
the New York cars
and the smoke from house
on fire close by.
The night ended
without ever dreaming.

The wail of sirens was knocking at the window
and again I dreamed about a quiet,
green field
and above it—
an unforgettable miracle in the sky—
the singing of a small lark.

<1984>

Translated by Ostap Kin and Ali Kinsella

Ліда Палій

Спекотливий день в Ню-Йорку

В кеньйонах міста
кам'яні доми
дихають один до одного
рибою і часником.
На асфальті
біля порожніх баньок із консервів
лежать худі коти, мов мертві.
При відкритих дверях
широкобедрі негритянки
сидять на сходах,
розставивши коліна.
Білими долонями
витирають піт з чола
й зорять туди,
де за іржавими драбинами
палає смуга розпеченого неба.
Темношкірі дітлахи
пищать під водоспадами
відкритих гідрантів.

<1960-ті>

Lydia Palij

A Hot Day in New York

In the canyons of the city,
the brownstones
breathe fish and garlic
on each other.
On the asphalt
near empty cans of food,
skinny cats rest like they're dead.
Wide-hipped black women
sit on the stoops
near open doors,
knees splayed apart.
They wipe the sweat from their brows
with their white palms
and gaze off to where,
beyond rusty fire escapes,
the line of burning sky blazes.
Dark-skinned kiddos
screech under the cascades
from the open hydrants.

<1960s>

Translated by Ostap Kin and Ali Kinsella

Дмитро Павличко

Повітря Нью-Йорка

Уста затули собі, очі заплющ —
Пучками пізнаєш повітря Нью-Йорка:
Притрушений сажею чорний плющ,
Тканина затуглого диму й мороку.
Ялини й берези на сухоти слабі,
а зорі, як діти в сиротинці, зачахли.
Ти звикаєш ковтати в безсилій злобі
Ганчір'я плюшевого вітру із кагли.
Наохрест на стрітах та авеню
Снують його вперто акулисті авта.
Ти всотаний в нього, немов у брехню,
Легені болять непомітно, як правда.
Ти в нього закручений, ніби в сувій,
Ти сохнеш у ньому, як труп фараона,
А дощик, як сльози з фарбованих вій, —
Нещира й нікчемна твоя оборона.
Ти бурі благаєш, чекаєш громів,
Обдурений хмарою підлогу смога.
Здається, нарешті ти зрозумів,
Що вбиває тебе найкрасніша дорога!

1967

Dmytro Pavlychko

New York's Air

Shut your mouth, close your eyes—
New York's air consists of clumps:
Soot-covered ivy you'll recognize,
A canvas of smoke above the dumps.
Consumptive and sick are birches and firs,
While stars like orphans do fade.
You learn to gulp with powerless rage
Plush rags of smokestack air.
Crisscrossing streets and avenues
Shark-cars weave through the air,
You're quite sucked in, in lies not a few,
Truth's pain your lungs must bear.
In its folds are you wrapped,
As a pharaoh's corpse quite dry,
Your useless defense as you stay trapped
Are tearful raindrops from painted eyes.
You pray that thunder and storm descend
From smog clouds of deceit.
And finally you comprehend
That this wondrous road is your death!

1967

Translated by Alexander Motyl

Іван Драч

Двоє ввечері пішки

«Олдсмобілі», «порше», «мустанги», «тріумфи»,
«пейсери», «мерседеси», «альфа-ромео», «піжо»,
летіли, мчали, ковзались, гальмували, зиріли,
мчали, сигналили, смерділи, сновигали, бігли,
всі дивились і всі не вірили, пропадом, пропадом,
мимо станцій Шелл, мимо станцій Ессо і Аполло,
мимо дерев забензинених, мимо станцій
                                    загазолінених
мчали машини, присвистували, аж вили,
крутили машини шиями, передніми фарами
                                    озирались,
що це за дві істоти Центральним парком увечері
не в машині і не в кареті, не у вертольоті і не в
                                    ракеті,
дві істоти просто на вулиці, просто на тротуарі,
дві істоти не їдуть, не летять, а, наче до нашої ери,
дві істоти пішки ідуть ввечері Центральним парком ...
озирались олдсмобілі, порше, мустанги,
                                    тріумфи,
крутили залізними шиями, жуйку собі жували,
ну й дивувались, лискучими шиями хитали,
«Емпайрстейт билдінг» нагнув неонову шию жирафи,
атомний підводний човен вилупив перескопи,
дві істоти пішки ідуть ввечері Центральним парком,
Армстронг з Місяця подивився і забув все на світі:
про літаючі блюдця і що треба на Землю вернуться.
Двоє ввечері пішки Центральним парком ...

<1975>

Ivan Drach

Two Walk in the Evening

Oldsmobiles, porsches, mustangs, triumphs,
pacers, mercedes, alfa romeos, peugeots,
flew, sped, skated, braked, watched.
sped, honked, stank, roved, ran,
everyone looked and no one believed, gone, gone,
past the Shell stations, past the Esso and Apollo stations
past the petrolled trees, past the gasolined stations
the cars sped, they whistled, nearly howled,
the cars craned their necks, they glanced 'round with their headlights,
who are these two creatures in Central Park in the evening,
not in a car, nor in a carriage, not in a helicopter, nor on a rocket,
two creatures just on the street, just on the sidewalk,
two creatures not riding, not flying but as if before our time
two creatures are walking in the evening in Central Park …
the oldsmobiles, porsches, mustangs, triumphs looked back,
they turned their iron necks, they chewed their gum,
and were surprised, they swayed their sleek necks,
the Empire State Building lowered its neon giraffe neck,
a nuclear submarine sent up its periscopes,
two creatures are walking in Central Park in the evening,
Armstrong looked down from the Moon and forgot everything in the world:
about flying saucers and that he must return to Earth.
Two walk in Central Park in the evening…

<1975>

Translated by Ostap Kin and Ali Kinsella

Нью-Йорк в стилі кубізму

Писано писання кубами хижими —
Лондонами, антверпенами, парижами,
Що записано, те записане, писане.
Навмисно писане. Зумисне писано. Миш не писне.

Кладено кладку. Складено складні складно.
Скло склеєне. Склепіння склепане.
Тужно обладнано. Натужно. Владно.
Одне, скорботне, марудне, хвалебне,

Розкотисте, жмотисте, щедре, щедротне
Котиться, крутиться, кротиться собвейно
Вільно і рвійно, невільне й запродане,
Супермодерне — смороднóмузейне …

Люблено й клято тебе на всі боки.
В ночах горобинних ти весь чорнобокий,
Немов заповзявся ти негром побути,
Усе проковтнувши — від Мао до Будди.

Кількоро доларів — й купили Манхеттен!
Де попіл вігвамів, які встигли зуміти,
Перкло яке розвергали шляхетне —
Чіпкі сталактити, круті сталагміти!

Чорна черінь у чернечім чорнилі
Все горне до себе й ковтає в горнилі …
Люто писане. Круто писане. Куб зумисне.
Кохане яке! Рідне яке! Яке ненависне!

Соняхом сонця стою на алфальті
І прозираю крізь джазове олово,
Як скрипка повисилась ніжно на альті,
Поклавши на плечі закохано голову.
Соняхом босим стою на Манхеттені.
Душа босоніж од сум'яття холоне …

New York in the Cubist Style

The writing is written in predatory cubes—
In Londons, Antwerps, Parises,
What is written is written, written down.
Written on purpose. Purposely written. A mouse's no kitten.

The bridge is built. The pieces are placed with poise.
The glass is glued. The vault is vaulted.
Woefully furnished. Staunchly. Ambitiously.
Alone, sorrowful, tedious, praised,

Reverberating, greedy, generous, bountiful, it
Wriggles, writhes, warrens like the subway
Freely and restless, arrested and sold off,
Super modern—museum stenchy…

They've loved and cursed you.
In the stormy nights you're black and blue
As if you decided to become a Negro,
Having swallowed everything—from Mao to Buddha.

A few dollars and they bought Manhattan!
Where's the dust of the wigwams that managed,
The noble hell they threw aside—
Stalactites that snag, stalagmites that stab!

Black oven bottom in the monk's ink
Rakes everything and swallows it in the stove…
Fiercely written. Sharply written. The cube is forced.
How lovely! How dear! How hated!

I stand on the asphalt like a sunflower of the sun
And I see through the jazzy tin,
How the violin amorously put its head on its
shoulders and hanged itself tenderly on the viola,
I'm stand in Manhattan like a barefoot sunflower.
My barefoot soul cools from the turmoil…

Куби оці планетою складені,
За душі задушені, за душі полатані,
О тоне прачорний, де ж ти, обертоне?!
Чом завжди ці кольори пересватані:
Де ніч горобина, там серце червоне!
Серце моє незнищенно червоне!

<1975>

These cubes are placed like a planet,
The souls strangled, the souls are mended
O tone so black, where are you, overtone?!
Why are these colors always matched.
When the night is stormy, the heart is red!
This heart of mine is indestructibly red!

<1975>

Translated by Ostap Kin and Ali Kinsella

Вічний блюз

Червоні троянди у чорному листі.
Фари червоні у чорному місті.
Губи червоні од пристрасті чорні,
Спалюють місто у чорному твісті.

Збілені білі — з безкров'я збілілі!
Червоні Гудзони в прачорному тілі!
Чорні до млості! Чорномажорні!
Вчаділі чорним! Громи почорнілі!

Чорне життя на білому світі —
Чорні попали до білих у сіті!
Та кажеш очима, як правдою в корені,
Білки в чорних білі, як фари нескорені!..

<1980>

Eternal Blues

Red roses in a black leaf.
Red headlights in a black city.
Red lips black with passion,
burn the city in a black twist.

Whitened whites are anemically whitened!
Red Hudsons in the old black body!
Black to fatigue! Black-and-positive!
Fumigated with black! Blackened thunders!

A black life in a white world—
the blacks fell into the whites' nets!
You say with your eyes like it's real truth
The blacks' squirrels are white like headlights unvanquished!...

<1980>

Translated by Ostap Kin and Ali Kinsella

Дмитрові Павличку

Це було в Нью-Йорку у собвеї —
Далеченько від землі своєї.
Йшли ми вдвох підземним переходом
Ввечері з намореним народом,
Що вертав додому по роботі
У задумі тлумній, у журботі.
А вгорі — казилися машини
Й місяць сяйвом мідної грошини
Захлинався від купюр неону,
Геть пірнав в масний собвей Гудзону.
Раптом — що це? Щось народ минає.
Може, це видіння чи мана є,
Але люд сахається і кроку
Наддає, щоб не вступить в мороку.
Та всього буває в переходах.
Бачимо, аж негр лежить на сходах.
Долілиць лежить, а хоче встати.
Ноги неслухняні, наче з вати.
Все як є. І кров. І звичний острах
Геть тікає в черевиках гострих.
Може б, ми теж прошмигнули мимо,
Але ж вдвох ішли ми незборимо,
Ледь перезирнулись — і до нього —
Лютого. Кривавого. Брудного.
Нас так вчили: люди, школа, мати,
Як людина впаде — підіймати.
Підіймаєм — він на нас як глипне,
Хто прилип — навіки той одлипне!
Як побачив, що це двійко білих,
Ще й таких нахабних, осмілілих,
Звівся п'яно, сивий і жорстокий —
Розметав нас люто на два боки!
Хто були йому ми? Комуністи?!
Просто — двоє білих, що полізти

From a poem "For Dmytro Pavlychko"

It was in the subway in New York—
Far away from our native land.
We two walked in the underground tunnel
In the evening with exhausted people
Going home after work
Lost in thought, in worry.
Above us the cars ran mad
And the moon, glowing like a copper penny,
Choked on the neon bills,
Dives into the greasy subway of the Hudson.
But what's it that? People are passing by.
Maybe it's an apparition or specter,
But people jump back and quicken
Their step lest they get into trouble.
Everything happens in the tunnels.
We see a black man lying on the stairs.
He's face down, but he wants to stand up.
His legs are disobedient as if made of cotton.
Everything is there. Blood. And the usual fear
Runs away in its pointy boots.
Perhaps we'd also speed on past,
But we two were walking invincibly,
We barely looked at each other—and approached him—
Ferocious. Bloody. Dirty.
They—people, school, mother—taught us
That if a person falls, pick them up.
We lift him and he stares at us
The one who stick to you won't let you go!
When he saw that we were white,
Impudent and those who dared
He, drunk, got up, grey and cruel—
He viciously threw us in two sides!
Who we were for him? Communists?
Just two white guys who were brave

Осмілили в його гето чорне —
Страдницьке, відрубне і відпорне.
Осторого! Стань ти нам на чати!
Джеймса Болдуїна варт читати,
Щоб відчути негритянський відрух,
Повен сопуху і повен вітру …

[…]

<1980>

Enough to enter his black ghetto—
Suffering, isolated, and resisting.
Caution! Stay and guard us!
It's time to read James Baldwin
To feel the African-American spirit
Full of fetor and full of wind ...

[...]

<1980>

Translated by Ostap Kin and Ali Kinsella

Борис Олійник

Від білої хати до Білого дому …

1. Знайомство

Сирий бетон аеропорту Кеннеді.
Якось зненацька вискнули шасі.
Все. Дев'ятнадцять десять за нью-йоркським.
… Давайте познайомимось, Америко.

Туман.
          Несе бензинним перегаром,
Немов сивухою від пияка.
На злітних смугах блимають вогні
Багрові і зелені. Потойбічно.
Задерши хижо вигнуті дзьоби,
Зловісно, важко в небо виповзають,
Немов доісторичні птерозаври,
Похмурі надсучасні літаки.
Ет цетера … Ет цетера.
(Набір джентельменський пристанційних вражень
короткочасних візитерів.)
Не звідси починається Америка.
Не з того боку починай знайомство …

Ти почни для знайомства
                    доскіпливий тест
Не з герба, що вінча
                    президентську карету,
Не з гучних Декларацій —
                    ми знаємо текст!
У двадцятім з підтексту
                    вивчають анкету.
Не з початку —
          з фіналу вивчати почни,
І початок розкриється,
                    наче долоня.
…Ось квадрат тишини.
                    Від стіни до стіни

152

Borys Oliynyk

From the cycle *From the White Home to the White House…*

1. Getting Acquainted

The gray concrete of Kennedy airport.
The chassis squeaks a bit abruptly.
That's it. Seven-ten New York time.
…Let's get acquainted, America.

Fog.
      It carries the boozy stench of gasoline,
Like rotgut from a drunkard.
The lamps glow on the runway
Scarlet and green. Otherworldly.
These gloomy, ultramodern aeroplanes,
Like prehistoric pterosaurs,
Curved beaks slash predatorily,
Ominously, they rise clumsily into the sky.
Et cetera… Et cetera.
(A gentlemanly collection of station impressions
from short-term visitors.)
This isn't where America begins.
Don't start getting acquainted from that side…

To get acquainted you take
      a comprehensive test
Not on the coat of arms that crowns
      the presidential motorcade
Not on the loud Declarations—
      we know the text!
In the twentieth century, they study the
      questionnaire from the subtext.
Not from the beginning,
      start studying from the end.
And the beginning will open
      like the palm of a hand.
…Here's your square of silence.
      From wall to wall

Вся Америка втислась
           в масштаб Арлінгтона.
Акуратно. І вулиці. Назви. Проспект.
Майже все, як в житті.
           Навіть краще, їй-богу …
Так себе планувала.
           Огляньте проект:
Видно задум
           і те, що лишилось від нього.
Все тут:
           замисли горді початку доби.
І — зола по замисленім,
           як від напалму.

От полеглі за волю —
           це засів судьби.
От врожай на сьогодні —
           убиті за В'єтнаму.
Понад ними —
           маленькі, лялькові хрести,
Як плюси до могил
           президентських
                 розкішних.
…От і перший підтекст.
           І — крути не крути,
Ну ніяк не збігається з текстами,
           грішний!

All of America squeezes into
        the space of Arlington.
Neatly. The streets. And names. And the boulevard.
Almost everything, like in life.
        Even better, by Jove!
It was planned that way.
        Take a look at the project:
The design is apparent
        as is what was left out.
It's all here:
        the proud beliefs from the start of the age.
And the ashes left behind,
        they could be from napalm.

And those who fell for freedom
        are the sowing of fate.
And today's harvest
        is the deaths in Vietnam.
Above them stand
        small, doll crosses,
Like plus signs to the graves
        of presidential
                luxuries.
… And here's the first subtext.
        And no matter how you spin it,
It doesn't line up with the texts,
        you sinner!

Translated by Ali Kinsella

2. Горить Нью-Йорк

Щоніч горить Нью-Йорк.
        Спливає кров'ю тьма.
Обличчя горожан — як лики, литі з воску.
І все довкруг космічний жах пройма,
Немов у видивах Ієроніма Босха.

Ти погуляв, Нью-Йорк!
        І от він — Страшний Суд:
Відьомське полум'я гуде в пекельнім танці,
Молись чи не молись: сувій гріхів несуть
Скальповані тобою індіанці.

Колись тобі, голодному, вони
Індика принесли, наївні діти честі.
Ти щедро відплатив:
        під регіт сатани
В серця їм розрядивши свій вінчестер!

…Горить, двигтить Нью-Йорк.
        Рокований огень
Висвітлює у цій містичній діорамі
Нелюдський сміх скальпованих племен,
Скляні зіниці вбитих у В'єтнамі.

Ну що, пожирував, всесвітній Вавилон?!
Тепер тремти і зри: у брамі Валтасара
Три слова начертав рокований вогонь,
Три віщі знаки грізної покари!

…Зійшли сирени на суцільний зойк.
Волають рації. Гуде юрба бентежно.
Це — страшний суд гряде …
        Але повір, Нью-Йорк:
Я руки не погрію на твоїй пожежі.

Я бачу, як нащадки перших вуглярів,
Сини ковбоїв — хлопці крутолобі —
На подив циніків-газетярів,
Несуть в огонь свої гаслярські роби.

2. New York Burns

New York burns every night.
     It bleeds darkness.
The urbanites' faces are visages poured from wax.
And a cosmic horror penetrates everything around
Like in Hieronymus Bosch's apparitions.

You've had your fun, New York!
     And here it is—Judgment Day:
The witch's fire hums in the hellish dance,
Pray or not: the scroll of sins is being carried
By the Indians you scalped.

Once they brought you, hungry,
A turkey, those naïve children of honor.
You paid them back generously:
     with a satanic laugh
You discharged your rifle into their hearts.

…New York burns, quakes.
     The inescapable fire
Illuminates in this mystical diorama
The bestial laughter of the scalped tribes,
The glassy pupils of those killed in Vietnam.

Well, have you had your fill, universal Babylon?!
Now tremble and behold: Balthazar's at the gates
The fire traced three inevitable words,
Three prophetic signs of the terrible punishment!

…The sirens have become a continuous wailing.
They call for reason. The masses drone anxiously.
This is it, Judgment Day is coming…
     But believe me, New York:
I won't warm my hands at your fire.

I see how the posterity of the first miners,
The sons of the cowboys—those sharp guys—
To the surprise of the cynics and newsies,
Wear their flameproof robes into the fire.

Ідуть порятувать не золоту мару,
Не гонор твій, підтятий Уотергейтом,
Не тайні списки в сейфах ЦРУ —
Таких уже демократичних стейтів!

Не за доляр, чорти його бери,
Що затулив, мов катаракта, скельця!
Урочо похили державні прапори:
Вони ідуть за тебе, люди серця!

Хтось обвуглів над жахо авеню …
Але в живий ланцюг
                                ступає інший вперто
І з рук до рук передає вогню
Твоє майбутнє, вирване у смерті.

В ручищах дублених, яким підкови гнуть,
Так ніжно й трепетно, мов хлібороб колосся,
Виносять з полум'я твого справдешню суть —
Дітей твоїх, Америко, виносять!

Крізь вогневу безумну, дику гру
Несуть, притисши до грудей могутніх.
І я в цім ланцюгу на руки їх беру
І впевнено передаю в майбутнє

Білявих, яко день, чорніших від ночей,
Червоних, як гранат, жовтіших од лимона —
Беру до рук твоїх дітей і в книзі їх очей
Читаю одсвіт сподівань Лінкольна.

…Коли розтане дим, і дощ паде з небес,
І, стерши піт, ми глянемо на себе, —
У серце нам кольне:
                                та ж ми стрічались десь …
Стривай, стривай, чи … не на кручах Ельби?

They go to save not the golden ghost,
Not your honor, cut down by Watergate,
Not the secret lists in the safes of the FBI—
These are democratic states after all!

Not for the greenbacks, devil take them,
That've clouded their lenses like cataracts!
National flags are beautifully lowered:
They're coming for you, people of the heart!

Some get horribly charred above the avenue…
But others obstinately
                    step forth into the living chain
And the fire passes from hand to hand
Your future, uprooted in death.

In cupped hands that bend horseshoes,
As tenderly and trembling as the sower, an ear of grain,
They bear your children, o America, out of the
Flames of your true essence. They bear them!

Through the fiery, mad, savage game
They carry them pressed to their powerful breasts.
And I, in this chain, take them by the hands
And pass them confidently into the future

The white as day, the black of night,
The red like the pomegranate, the lemon yellow—
I take your children in my arms and in the book of their eyes
I read the light of Lincoln's hopes.

…When the smoke clears and the rain falls from the heavens,
And we wipe away our sweat and take a look at ourselves
We'll feel a stab in our hearts:
                    haven't we met somewhere…
Hold on, hold on, was it not… on the cliffs of the Elbe?

Translated by Ali Kinsella

4. Прометей приручений

Якось Нью-Йорком,

крізь ядуху сперту,

Я брів, мов Дант, в сірчанім тумані.

І раптом на скалі Рокфеллер-центру

Сам Прометей — свят-свят! — явивсь мені.

Я вже хотів у ноги Богоборцю

В священній шані пасти долілиць.

Та щось мені спинило на півкроці,

І зник міраж, як пил з-під колісниць.

Ні скелі, ні орла.

Отямивсь: де я?!

На тлі стіни, як в дзеркалі кривім,

Блаженно возлежав із ликом Прометея

Золочений лінивий херувим.

З-під банку зиркав іронічно стражник.

Мовляв, за гроші … й не таких, либонь.

…І крикнув ридма я відступникові:

— Зрадник!

Ну, сам продавсь…

Так як ти міг — вогонь?!

Ти ж правив у змаганнях нам на міру.

Таж поруч тебе сам Іуда — тінь:

Той — одного продав…

А ти ж запродав віру

Мою і всіх минулих поколінь! —

І камінь взяв я, гострий і ребристий.

Вже замахнувсь…

Та раптом височінь

Хитнулася,

і з металевим свистом

На голову мені поверглась тінь:

Над хмарочосом, що нависнув грізно:

Уп'явши кігті у криваву плоть,

4. Prometheus Doomed

Across New York,
      through the thick, stale air
I once trudged like Dante in the sulfuric fog.
When suddenly on a rock in front of Rockefeller Center
Prometheus himself—holy, holy!—appeared before me.

I wanted to graze at the feet of the Theomachist
Prostrate in his blessed aureole.
Yet something stopped me in my tracks,
And the mirage vanished like dust from under a chariot.

Neither rocks, nor eagles.
      I came to: Where am I?!
Reflected in the wall, like in a funhouse mirror,
Was a gilded, indolent cherub
Lying blissfully like Prometheus.

A guard stared sardonically from the bank.
As if, need money? I've seen worse…
…and sobbing, I shouted at the defector:
                  "Traitor!"
He's the one who sold out…
          How could you—for fire?!

You ruled us equitably in the competitions
Judas himself stands beside you—a mere shadow:
He sold one man…
           But you sold the faith
Of me and all previous generations!

And I took up the stone, sharp and serrated.
I'd already raised my hand…
      When suddenly the skies
Bowed down,
    and with a metallic whistle
Smote my head with their shadow:

Above the skyscrapers hanging menacingly:
Its claws dug into the bloody flesh,

Летів орел
                похмуро і залізно
Чинити кару за Евксинський Понт.

І стогін болю із гірського краю,
Протявши небо,
                     вмерз у материк:
— Мужайтесь, люди! Я за вас вмираю,
Та доки люди ви —
                 не вмру повік!

І зник фальшивий дубль,
                 як потороча.
І я одкрив у древньому
                 нове:
— Покіль за нас вмираєш,
                 Богоборче, —
Безсмертний ти,
                 бо віра в нас живе.

An eagle flew
       gloomy and steely
To exact punishment for the Black Sea.

And a moan of pain from the craggy land,
Cut through the sky
              and froze on the mainland:
"Man up, people! I am dying for you,
But as long as you're human,
          I shall never die!"

And the false double disappeared
          like a spook.
And I discovered in antiquity
          something new:
"As long as you're dying for us,
          O theomachist,
you are immortal,
      for our faith is alive.

Translated by Ali Kinsella

5. Та від Білої хати …

Та від Білої хати
            аж до Білого дому —
Субмарини й ракети,
            океани, туман і печаль …
Принеси мені вітре,
            хоч стеблину соломи
З материнського поля
            на свинцевий Гудзонів причал.

В цім залізному світі
            верховодять машини.
В темних вигинах вулиць
            бродить ніж та оптичний приціл …
Принеси мені, вітре,
            сизий холод ожини,
В цю задушливу ніч
            принеси мені сонце в руці.
Тут безжалісно правлять
            навіть з сонця проценти …
А душа моя вдома,
            а душа моя шлях обійма,
Де стрічаєш ти, мамо,
            поштаря із райцентру,
А листа все немає,
            а листа щось від сина нема …
Не тужи, моя мамо,
            при вікні,
                  при віконці —
Понад океани,
            великі й малі,
Наша вишня на гілці
            подає мені сонце,
Що ніколи не зайде,
            бо зіходить на отчій землі.
Я до рідного сонця
            прихиливсь, як до брата.

5. From the White Home...

From the White Home
                    all the way to the White House
Submarines and rockets,
                    oceans, fog, and sorrow...
Bring me, o wind,
                    at least one piece of straw
From my native fields
                    to the Hudson's leaden wharf.

In this iron world
                    cars are in command.
In the dark bends of the streets
              the knife and the optical sight roam...
Bring me, o wind,
                    the blue-gray cold of blackberries
Into this stifling night
                    bring me the sun in your hand.
Here they ruthlessly demand
                    interest even from the sun...
But my soul is at home,
                    and my soul embraces the path,
Where you, mom, meet
                    the mailman from town,
But the letter's not there,
              the letter from your son's not there...
Don't grieve, dear mother,
            near the window,
                    near the little window—
Across the oceans,
            large and small,
Our cherry on the branch
                    gives me a sun,
That will never set,
            for it rises on my paternal land.
I nestled up to my sun,
            as if to my own brother.

Хмарочоси щезають,
            ніби ящери, в темінь століть …
Вища Білого дому
            моя Білая хата,
Бо за правду стоїть.
            Бо на правді одвіку стоїть.

1978

The skyscrapers vanish,
>   like lizards into the darkness of the ages…
My White Home is,
>   higher than the White House,
For it stands for truth.
>   For it has always stood in truth.

1978

Translated by Ali Kinsella

Part III: 1990s–2016

Абрам Кацнельсон

Уолл-стріт

Так наче створювали гето нам —
від нас ізолювали світ.
І от іду тепер Манхеттеном,
переді мною Уолл-стріт.

Про Уолл-стріт, немов чудовисько,
чимало чули реплік злих:
мовляв, ото осердя утиску
і всяких планетарних лих.

І згадуючи про химери ці,
було нам соромно, коли
реальність бачачи в Америці,
цією вулицею йшли.

Ще нас лякали хмарочосами.
А я повз них не раз ходив —
радів творінням рук і розуму,
красі струнких висотних див.

Та все ж і тут, за океаном ми —
серед рекламних веремій —
в душі лишаємось киянами,
залюблені в Хрещатик свій …

1995

Abram Katsnelson

Wall Street

It's like they made a ghetto for us—
they isolated the world from us.
So now I'm walking around Manhattan,
And Wall Street lies before me.

About Wall Street, like about a beast,
we've heard a lot of nasty comments:
like, it's the center of oppression
and various worldly calamities.

And recalling these illusions,
we felt ashamed when
we saw the American reality
as we walked down this street.

They tried to scare us with skyscrapers.
But I've gone past them many times.
I enjoyed these creations of hands and minds,
the beauty of these tall, slender miracles.

But even here, across the ocean,
among the noise of ads,
in our souls we remain Kyivans,
in love with our Khreshchatyk.

1995

Translated by Ostap Kin and Ali Kinsella

На Бродвеї

На рекламно залитому сяйвом Бродвеї,
наче Богом врятовані, ходять євреї.
Де звелись хмарочоси стрункими огромами,
йдуть оті, що вночі сни їх будять погромами.
Йде старий інвалід з перекошеним ротом,
що роздраний був у концтаборі дротом.
В того спалено діда живцем в крематорії.
А онук батьком став, порівнявся із Торою.
Капелюх, довгі пейси. І з ним, поруч матері,
по ранжиру йдуть чада. І їх уже п'ятеро.

На рекламно залитому сяйвом Бродвеї,
наче Богом врятовані, ходять євреї …

1998

On Broadway

On Broadway, illuminated by ads aglow,
as if saved by God, the Jews, they all stroll.
They who are awakened by pogroms at night
move past the skyscrapers clustered so tight.
An old cripple walks with them, mouth split and splayed,
it was slashed at a concentration camp with a blade.
That one's granddaddy burned alive in an oven.
Grandson's now a father and lets the Torah govern.
A hat and long sidelocks. With him and their mother,
their brood walks along—all five, one after another.

On Broadway, illuminated by ads aglow,
as if saved by God, the Jews, they all stroll…

1998

Translated by Ostap Kin and Ali Kinsella

Сергій Жадан

Нью-Йорк — факін сіті

ніби не вода ніби не витікала
не збивала з ніг не холонула на камінні
лише закинутий на хідники під
аритмічну музику і веселі піднебесся
я знаю — годі щось винести із такого досвіду
коли придорожня оса перелітає за вікном у південному напрямку
і незалежні радіостанції першими сповіщають
про наближення міста

вже тоді як псується погода
ні везіння тобі не буде ні заспокоєння хоча ніби

так мало статись
із-за рогу вибрідає юний трансвестит
в довгому дощовику і теплій спідниці
стоїть перед своїм під'їздом шукає ключі дощ тече обличчям
фарба збивається під очима наче бруд під нігтями
великі сині краплі скочуються на тонкі вилиці
на в'язаний одяг і чорні ботинки

ніби і справді не лишилось слідів
і пам'ять ніби не вода і не холоне глибоко в тілі
любов до великих населених пунктів
ніби любов до дерев що ростуть незалежно від тебе
говориш собі засинаєш непомітно
і очі закочуються під повіки
наче згублені іграшки

<2001>

Serhiy Zhadan

New York Fuckin' City

as if water wasn't pouring down
growing cold on the cement knocking people off their feet
just tossing me down on the sidewalk
to arrhythmic music and blissful heavens
I know—it's hard to learn anything from experiences like these
a roadside wasp flies by the window heading south
as an independent radio station announces
that you're approaching the city

when the weather turns bad
there's no luck or peace although both were promised
a young transvestite emerges from around the corner
in a long rain coat and a warm skirt
stops at the front door looking for keys rain pouring down her face
the makeup cakes under her eyes like dirt under nails
great blue drops run down her narrow cheeks
onto woolen clothes and black boots

as if indeed no trace remained
and memory wasn't water and wasn't growing cold deep inside the body
love of large cities
is like the love of trees that grow without you
you say to yourself as you imperceptibly fall asleep
and your eyes roll up behind the lids
like lost toys

<2001>

Translated by Virlana Tkacz and Wanda Phipps

* * *

І найменша дівчинка в Чайна-тауні,
і старі баптисти в холодних церквах Мангетена
навіть не уявляють, які зірки падають в наші комини,
і яке смарагдове часникове листя
росте на наших футбольних полях.
Це ось океан, без початку і кінця,
заливає берег, на якому стоять китайські їдальні,
і тисяча кашалотів ховається в ньому за піском і мулом,
навіки відділяючи мене від країни,
яку я любив.
Це ось чорні дерева в холодних снігах,
ніби африканки на білих простирадлах,
і на кожному дереві сидять птахи,
крикливі птахи еміграції,
співучі птахи вигнання.
А це ось я
кожної ночі
вві сні
вантажу свій пароплав зорями і пшеницею,
заповнюю трюми ромом і цикутою,
прогріваю старі машини,
так як топлять кахляні печі.
Вже зовсім скоро Господь покличе нас усіх,
поверне океанські потоки, пожене нас у темряву.
Ридай тоді за мною,
солодка морська капусто Америки,
так як умієш лише ти одна,
так як умієш лише ти одна.

2008

* * *

And the smallest little girl in Chinatown,
and the old Baptists in the cold churches of Manhattan
don't even imagine how the stars fell into our chimneys,
and how emerald leaves of garlic
grow on our soccer pitches.

This is ocean, without beginning or end,
flooding the shore where Chinese buffets stand
and a thousand sperm whales hide beneath sand and silt
separating me forever from the country
I loved.

Here are black trees in cold snow,
like African women on white blankets,
and birds sit in every tree,
the vehement birds of emigration,
the melodious birds of exile.

And here I am
every night
in my dream
I load my steamship with stars and wheat,
I fill holds with rum and hemlock,
I warm up old engines
the way you stoke tile stoves.

Yet soon the Lord will summon us all,
will divert the oceans' tides, will urge us into darkness.
Then weep for me,
sweet seaweed of America,
the way only you can do it,
the way only you can do it.

2008

Translated by Ostap Kin

Оксана Забужко

New York, NY

… Так довго знати країну, що пам'ятати часи,
Коли проїзд на метро був удвічі дешевшим …

В небі горять перехняблені Терези,
І Стрілець з цього боку Землі виглядає, як вершник.
Місяць з'являється нагло, мов терорист, —
Не з того боку, і не за тим закрутом …
В цій країні я вільна — як вільним буває лист,
У шухляду вкинутий і до пори забутий.
Можна звернути з шляху і в парку на Ріверсайд
Хоч до ранку сидіти і просто дивитись на Бруклін …
(В цій країні й без мене повнісінько всяких зайд,
На краях їх зору я лиш ще одна «біла кукла».)

Анонімність і є свобода — не краденого «ай-ді»,
А лишень непотрібного, навіть в нічнім мотелі, —
Відчуття під ногами не тверді і не води, —
А колишньої стелі.
От задля цього й долається океан
(Й виставляються Вежі, як кеглі, — на те, щоб збити …).
Я люблю цю країну — за те, що вона нічия,
Що вона не моя — і не мушу її любити.

2002

Oksana Zabuzhko

New York, NY

…you've known the country so long you can remember
when the subway cost half as much…

Tilted Libra burns in the sky, and
from this hemisphere Sagittarius looks like a cowboy.
the Moon appears abruptly like a terrorist,

not from her usual side, but around a foreign corner…
In this country I'm free, just like a letter
tossed into a drawer and forgotten until its time.
You can veer from your route and sit in the park on Riverside
until morning, just gazing at Brooklyn…
(Even before me, this country held enough unwelcomes—
in whose eyes I am just another white chick.)

Anonymity is freedom—even before an ID is stolen,
it's extraneous, even at a motel—
what you tread is neither firmament, nor waters,
it's what used to be the ceiling.
This is why the ocean is crossed
(and the Towers are set up, like pins to be knocked over).
I love this country because it's nobody's,
because it is not mine and I don't have to love it.

2002

Translated by Ostap Kin, Ali Kinsella and Jazlyn Kraft

Юрій Андрухович

Bombing New York City

Осіб жіночої статі запрошуємо на вихід —
Зникнути в темряві.
Цей номер — суто наш, чоловічий.
Зрештою, так захотіла природа,
Саме цю непотрібну стать, наділивши здатністю
Без води гасити жевріючі багаття.

Небо над нами в зірках.
Це серпень, серпень.
Місто під нами прекрасне, ніби Галактика.
Це серпень, серпень.
Це багаття, при якому щойно сиділи.

«Це Нью-Йорк, — кажу я. —
Приготуватись до бомбардування».
Починаємо неводночас, але всі четверо.
Струмені перехрещуються,
Місто під нами сичить
І гасне цілими кварталами.

«Більше уваги Мангеттену, — кажу я. —
Чорний Гарлем і Бронкс не чіпаємо».
«З Брукліном і Квінсом покінчено», —
Доповідає Джон, дещо п'яніший і зосередженіший.

Поваливши Крайслер, Сіґрам та Емпайр Стейт,
Ми в цілому задоволені операцією.
Затягуємо замки на ширіньках,
Відходимо на базу, в темряву,
Почуваючись небесними асами.

Мине місяць —
І такі жарти видадуться поганими.

<2004>

Yuri Andrukhovych

Bombing New York City

Those of the female gender are requested to leave—
to disappear into the darkness.
This is a guy thing.
It's how nature herself planned it,
bestowing on this useless gender the ability
to put out smouldering bonfires without water.

The sky above us is starry. It's August, August.
The city below us as gorgeous as the Galaxy.
It's August, August.
This is the bonfire, which we were sitting around just now.

"It's New York"—I say.—
"Prepare for bombing."

We start, not at the same time,
but all four of us. The streams cross,
the city beneath us hisses and whole neighbourhoods
go out.

"More attention to Manhattan"—I say.—
"Black Harlem and the Bronx are not to be touched."
"Brooklyn and Queens are down"—
adds John,
a bit drunker and more concentrated.

Having demolished Chrysler, Seagram and the Empire State,
we are generally satisfied with the operation.
We pull up our zips, we go back
to base, in darkness, feeling like the aces of creation.

One month later—
such jokes are in bad taste.

<2004>

Translated by Sarah Luczaj

Василь Махно

Нью-йоркська листівка Богданові Задурі

хотів надіслати тобі листівку з Бруклінським мостом
і не знайшов у крамниці
в Америці також не все є

натомість знайшов листівку з Джоном Ешбері з 60-их

і мимоволі порівняв його з тим якого я бачив на 22-й вулиці у його
    помешканні
коли Джон до кінця не зрозумів звідки в Україні беруться поети

заплативши 70 центів
здивованому крамареві в якого ніхто ніколи не купував фотолистівки
    поетів
заховав у внутрішню кишеню піджака

і пішов у напрямку Бродвею

потім звернув і побачив Бруклінський міст

чи тобі цікава ця нью-йоркська топографія?

бо в Нью-Йорку ніколи не загубишся
але чи віднайдеш себе?
що за лабіринти вони тут понабудовували?
ці канали прорито бульдозерами — скелі підірвано динамітом

тут вистарчає
співаків — матросів — повій — гебреїв — афроамериканців які у
    кожному рядку *Поета у Нью-Йорку* Лорки
що шукав тут сексуальних пригод у той час коли все пішло шкереберть
1929 року коли збанкрутувала Біржа
може тому він відплив згодом на Кубу
а може тому що не вивчивши англійської йому ставало щораз сумніше і
    самотніше?

я хотів надіслати тобі Бруклінський міст: бо він наче жест вилинялої дівки
    — статуї Свободи — позеленілої від океанічної вологости яку всадили на
штучному острові та яка стількох обдурила

хіба можна вірити продажним дівкам?

Vasyl Makhno

New York Postcard to Bohdan Zadura

I wanted to send you a postcard with the Brooklyn Bridge
and I couldn't find one in the store
America does not have everything either

instead I found a postcard with John Ashbery from the 60s

and in spite of myself compared him to the same one I saw on 22nd Street in
his apartment
when John failed to understand where poets in Ukraine come from

having paid the 70 cents
to the surprised merchant who had never had anyone buy from him a postcard
with the photo of a poet
I tucked it into the inner pocket of my jacket

and went in the direction of Broadway

then I turned and saw the Brooklyn Bridge

does this New York topography interest you?

because in New York you will never get lost
but will you find yourself again?
what sort of labyrinths have they built here?
these canals were bulldozed,
the towers were dynamited

here, there are enough
singers—sailors—prostitutes—Jews—African-Americans that can be found
in every
line of Lorca's *Poet in New York*
who was searching for sexual adventures here at a time when everything went
topsy-turvy
in 1929 when the stock market crashed
maybe that is why he ended up sailing off to Cuba
or maybe because not having learned English he became sadder
and lonelier?

I wanted to send you the Brooklyn Bridge because it's like the gesture
of a washed up broad—

Інколи на Ґринвіч-Вілідж збираються поети посидіти у якісь каварні щоби читати вірші
але якось нудно вони це роблять наче жують жуйку

кажуть: що всі тут еміґранти

і мандрівці

і шукачі пригод:

як Ґомбрович який більше залишив автографів у Буенос-Айресі на
    квитанціях Banco Polaco
аніж понаписував текстів

як Віткаци — вічний турист і мешканець Закопаного — який невідомо
    для чого коли почалася війна поїхав до Перемишля (чи десь у тих
    околицях) і там наклав на себе руки

як Бруно Шульц із простреленою потилицею біля цинамонової крамниці
на одній із вуличок Дрогобича який не встиг виконати наказ німецького
    вояка
залишив малюнки та фрески — працю гімназіяльного вчителя і свої
еротичні марення

чому ми всі еміґранти?

Господи — колись вигукнув Збіґнєв Герберт — *дивуюся що світ такий
різноманітний*

і я дивуюся також кожного разу зустрічаючи цих доходяг-гіпі —
    розмальованих панків — місцевих алкоголіків які обсикають крамниці
і яких не арештовує поліція

споглядаю:
нічні вогні великого міста — вони горять хутром небесного лиса

Підземки які стрясаються від руху потягів
і звучать музикою різних етносів що стікає разом із каналізаційними
    водами

цих голодних карибських жінок які потрясають цицьками та бедрами
— цих сухих і вицвілих англосаксонок які мов жердини встромлені на
вулицях замість дерев як ліхтарі та світлофори

чи тобі цікаві ці нью-йоркці?

ці ритми — ці звуки?

the Statue of Liberty—a fading green from the ocean clamminess who was perched
onto a faux island and who has fooled so many

One can't really trust girls for sale, can one?

sometimes poets gather in Greenwich Village to sit in some coffeehouse
in order to read poetry
but they go about it in a bored sort of way
as though they were chewing gum

they say: everyone here is an immigrant

and a wanderer

and an adventure-seeker:

like Gombrowicz who left behind more autographs in Buenos Aires on
the tickets of Banco Polaco
than written texts

like Witkacy—the eternal tourist and resident of Zakopane who for some
reason when the war began went to Przemysl (or thereabouts) and laid hands
on himself

like Bruno Schulz with his temple shot through next to the cinnamon shop on
one of the narrow streets of Drohobych who failed to execute the order of the
German soldier and left behind paintings and frescoes—the work of a gymna-
sium teacher and his own erotic musings

why are we all immigrants?

Lord—once Zbigniew Herbert shouted—*I am surprised that the world is so
diverse*

and I am awed as well every time I run into those hippie street people—
the painted fags—local alcoholics—who piss up stores and who the police fail
to arrest

I observe:
the nocturnal fires of a big city—they burn with the pelt of a celestial fox

the subways that jolt and jostle from the motion of the trains
and resound with the music of diverse ethnicities that drips down along with
the water rushing through the canals

those hungry Caribbean women that shake their tits and hips—those desiccated

ти пам'ятаєш що є ще ці провінційні містечка збудовані за Маґдебурзьким
    правом
із площею яка неодмінно називається Ринок
церквами й костелами — поруйнованими синагогами

чи вони — у затисненій долоні Бруно Шульца — нагадують маленьке
ластів'я?
чи він устиг тоді схопити тінь пір'їн?

пригадую собі пагорби Бучача:
на центральній вулиці ще залишилися крамниці з кованими дверми
і старими замками роботи місцевих ковалів

гебрейський цвинтар на якому плити з написами на івриті — наче книга
родів галицьких гебреїв —

чи не про той Бучач писав Шмуель Аґнон?

чи не той Бучач я шукав разом із його дочкою Емою Ярон на вцілілих
рештках гебрейського цвинтаря у Тернополі
а французьке телебачення знімкувало коли вона пальцем протирала затерті
й позеленілі літери на могильній плиті якогось свого далекого родича?
і притулившись до неї довго щось шепотіла

чому Бруклінський міст такий короткий і чому ним не можна доїхати до
Європи?

чому пам'ять така довга і довжина її вимірюється нескінченністю?

я звичайно знайду цю листівку — а ти коли купиш авто виїжджай на
Бруклінський міст біля Пулав
і прямуй до Нью-Йорка

посидимо на Ґринвіч-Вілідж
і почитаємо одне одному вірші

бо їхня мить (і наша також) як у нічних мотилів
і від того — що присвітиш комусь — не стає легше

<2004>

and withered anglosaxonites that stick out like poles on the streets like streetlamps instead of trees

are these newyorkers interesting to you?

these rhythms—these sounds?

you remember there are still those provincial towns built according to the Magdeburg Law
with the open area, the square, uniformly called the *Rynok*
with the churches and the kostels and the ruined synagogues
do they—in Bruno Schulz's tightly curled palm—recall a tiny sparrow?
did he manage then to grasp the shadow of their feathers?

I recall the hills of Buchach
on the central streets there still remain shops with wrought iron doors
and ancient castles fashioned by local blacksmiths

the Jewish cemetery on which the tombstones are written in Hebrew—as though a book of the genesis of Galician Jews—

was it not this Buchach of which wrote Shmuel Agnon?

is it not the same Buchach I searched together with his daughter Emuna Yaron
in the surviving remains of the Hebrew cemetery in Ternopil
as the French television channel showed as she fingered the faded
and greening letters upon the gravestone of one of her distant relatives?
and drawing closer, persisted in whispering something extensively

why is the Brooklyn bridge so short and why doesn't it go
to Europe?

why is memory so elongated and why is its length measured in endlessness?

of course I'll find that postcard and when you buy your car
get off at the Brooklyn Bridge near Pulawy
and head to New York

we'll sit in Greenwich Village
and read each other poems

for their moment—(and ours as well) as in nocturnal butterflies
and from this—that you may enlighten someone—it doesn't get easier

<2004>

Translated by Luba Gawur

На каві у «Starbucks»

у грудні — у долішньому нью-йорку —
            п'ючи каву в «Starbucks» — спостерігаю
як два мексиканці вкладають мармурові плити
            до парадного входу в будинок

у кав'ярні крутять нав'язливий Jingle bells
вулицями миготять нью-йоркці
            з різдвяними подарунками й авта
вуличні торговці розпродують туристам усілякий непотріб
поліціянти мирно дрімають у теплому авті
до церкви черга — ні,
            сьогодні не неділя — відкриття якоїсь виставки

ну, ось і 12-й апостол року —
            грудень сідає за стіл тайної вечері
нещедрі плоди твоїх днів викладеш із пакета
            щоб пригостити 12 апостолів
по дорозі забіг до крамниці та купив нашвидкуруч
але вони знають усе
і ви мовчки разом доїсте прісний хліб завершення року

ну, ось і надходить час
            коли згірклий досвід плодів і скисле молоко днів
усе частіше з'являються на твоєму щоденному столі
коли шум океану все частіше висить у просторі твоїх слів
усе частіше ти дріботиш п'ятилітнім до кошари
                        щоби подихати випарами
овець бо — казали — відпустить твій сухий кашель

ну, ось ти — сорокалітній мужчина — ще укладаєш слова
ще записуєш їх — що ж тут нового?
з античних часів лише кільком
            удалося переплисти океан тисячоліть

сьогодні — разом із тобою
            100 тисяч поетів укладають словники своєї мови
чи хоч уламок строфи допливе (якщо буде куди плисти)
чи хоч звук твоєї мови —

Coffee in Starbucks

in december—in downtown new york—
                    drinking coffee in Starbucks—i watch
two mexicans laying marble wall slabs
                            in the entrance to the building

an irksome Jingle Bells keeps playing in the café
new yorkers shimmer with their christmas gifts and cars
street peddlers sell the tourists all kinds of crap
the policemen snooze peacefully in their warm car
there's a line to get into a church—no, today's not Sunday—
                            the opening of some exhibit

well, here's the twelfth apostle of the year—
            december is sitting down at the table of the last supper
from the bag you unpack the meager fruits of your days
                                to host the twelve apostles
on my way i ran into a store and hastily bought them
but they know everything
and in silence you'll finish eating the unleavened bread
                                    of the year's end

well, the time is approaching when the bitter experience
            of the fruits and the soured milk of your days
appear all the more often on your daily table
when the sound of the ocean all the more often
                        hangs in the space of your words
all the more often like a five-year-old you take small steps
                    to the sheepfold to breathe the sheep exhalations
because—they say—it will relieve your dry cough

well, here you are—a forty-year-old man—
                    you're still composing words
you're still scribbling them down—what else is new here?
from ancient times only a few managed to float
                        across the ocean of millennia
today—together with you a hundred thousand poets
                    are composing dictionaries of their language
at least the debris of a strophe will float its way

за законами астрономії — уподібнюючися звізді —
якої вже нема — (якщо ті закони не брехливі)

ну, ось виживаєш останні дні старого року —
наче оплачений готельний номер —
попиваєш каву — і дивишся як:
два мексиканці — розпилюють камінь —
обидва підносять його — допасовуючи до стіни —
знову поволі опускають і знову надпилюють

камінь тяжкий

життя легке

<2004>

(if there'd be a way to float somewhere)
at least the sound of your language—according to the laws
        of astronomy—becoming like a star—
that no longer is — (if those laws aren't wrong)

well, here you're using up the last days of the old year—
        like a hotel room you've already paid for—
you drink up the coffee—and watch:

two mexicans—cutting the stone slab—
both of them lift it up—fitting it to
the wall—again they slowly lower it and again they cut it

the stone slab is heavy

life is easy

<2004>

Translated by Michael M. Naydan

Federico Garcia Lorca

Хто вилизує теплий жовток місяця
хто пише про короля Гарлему
забувши принца Гамлета
хто заповідає зеленим деревам
їх зелену смерть

і тремтливим словам
їх смерть
тремтливу?

місто яке він пив — мов вино —
витекло крізь діряві отвори його жил
дрантливий папір
всмоктав чорнило — не залишаючи написаних слів —
усі флейти своїми
металевими кишками
переварили повітря на нікчемні звуки
а з картин Далі повирізували шлуночки серця

однак він міг оповідати усім про місто в якому
хірургічне втручання поета
необхідне
як пожежникам
потрібно більше води
— сечі у міхурах —
— слини у роті —

у його місті мешкали крокодили і повії —
зелені іґуани і хори афроамериканців
він доїзджав до Гарлема поїздом
і дивився на короля
який палив кубинські сиґари
і пускав колами дим наказуючи своїм підлеглим
не чіпати цього іноземця

він записував назви каварень і театрів
вчив напам'ять числа вулиць
носив альпійські гірські костюми
платив музи́кам завжди більше аніж вони того заслуговували

Federico Garcia Lorca

Who licks up the warm yolk of the moon
who writes about the king of Harlem
having forgotten prince Hamlet
who prophesies to green trees
their green death

and to trembling words
their trembling death?

the city he imbibed—like wine—
leaked out through the apertures of his porous veins
shoddy paper
sucked in the ink—obliterating the written words—
all the flutes with their
metallic intestines
contorted the air into awful sounds
and from Dali's paintings cut out the ventricles from the heart

he could however tell everyone stories about the city in which
surgical intrusion by a poet
is as indispensable as
plentiful water is for firemen
—or urine is for bladders—
—or saliva for a mouth—

in his city resided crocodiles and whores—
green iguanas and choruses of African-Americans
he commuted to Harlem by subway
and watched the king
who smoked Cuban cigars
and blew rings of smoke ordering his underlings
not to bother this foreigner

he recorded the names of coffee houses and theaters
memorized street numbers
wore Tyrolean attire
always paid musicians more than they deserved

and listened to jazz as if bewitched

слухав джаз мов заворожений
коли саксофоніст
виціловуючи лебедину шию саксофона
виблискував золотими браслетами
і коштовними перснями

він слухав джаз у Cotton Club

У Гарлемі
під кінець 20-тих
джаз-клуби множились
наче повії і моряки
у портових містах

<2007>

when a saxophonist
smothering with kisses the swan-shaped neck of the saxophone
would flash his gold bracelets
and precious rings

he listened to jazz at the Cotton Club

In Harlem
towards the end of the '20s
jazz clubs were multiplying
like whores and sailors
in port cities

<2007>

Translated by Orest Popovych

Прощання з Брукліном

Я записую кілька слів у розбухлу книгу прощань
сидячи біля бухти овечої голови — п'ючи — між уривками — чай
і бруклинським чайкам кирилицю на серветці
залишу на пам'ять — вона їм …
але обопільна залежність — себто життя навзаєм
підтверджується прислів'ям: *де тонко — там рветься*

що їм — зрештою — до моїх европ — індій — авіаліній
відчіплених парусів з яхт — світла розпорошеного в насінні
поржавілого металу моїх же конструкцій
віршів — блошиного ринку вживаних велосипедів
коні айленду записаного на касеті
дами з собачкою — вірніше суки при сучці

вони що пахнуть океаном і бухтою овечої голови
залітають найдальше до Флетбуш — минають сабвею рови
і ловлять потік повітря — в напрямку на коні айленд
рослаблюють крила вітрові на поталу
і долітають до бухти — наче концертну залу
заповнюють в білих смокінгах — але

ресторанна музика глушить їх крик і королівський почет
лабухи по-російськи лабають до пізньої ночі
й підпилі коханці в засклених мерседесах
втікають неначе на них влаштували погоню
чайки осіли на яхтах — і їх вже ніхто не гонить
хіба що проспівана фраза *«ах мама моя одесса»*

турецька чайна також зачиняється — власник дрімає
сьогодні клієнтів обмаль — один ще чогось чекає
пише щось на серветці — креслить — скоріше б забрався
російськомовні євреї справляють весілля
заблудлий хасид під стіною — неначе месія —
затуляє собою напис *«тут були ваня і вася»*
бруклин церков православних синагог і мечетей
бруклин китайців індусів — учень і вчитель
власнику чайни — здається — ввірвася терпець
він посміхаючись каже *right now is close*

A Farewell to Brooklyn

in my bulging book of farewells I write down a few words
sitting near Sheepshead Bay—drinking tea—between the excerpts
and to Brooklyn seagulls I'll leave on a napkin
my Cyrillic writing as a memento—for them prepared…
but our mutual dependence—meaning the life we had shared
is confirmed by the adage: *a chain breaks at its weakest link*

besides—what do they care—about my Europes—Indias—airlines
the sails detached from yachts—the light scattered in the see—
about the rusty metal in my own structures of verses—
a flea market of used bicycles
about the play "Coney Island" recorded on DVD
about "A Lady with a Dog"—more precisely a bitch with a bitch

they who smell of the ocean and of the bay of sheepsheads
fly at most as far as Flatbush—passing by the subway tracks
and catch the air stream—in the direction of Coney Island
falling prey to the wind they exhaust their wings
and arrive at the bay—as if filling a concert hall
in their white evening jackets—but

the restaurant music muffles their shrieks and royal retinue
musicians play Russian songs late into the night
and tipsy lovers inside their dimmed Mercedeses
slip away as if escaping pursuit
the gulls have settled on the yachts—no one pursues them any more
except perhaps for the refrain *"oh my mama Odessa"*

the Turkish tearoom is closing too—its owner napping
few customers today—just this one who's still lingering
he writes on a napkin—then crosses it out—I wish he'd disappear
as Russian Jews are celebrating a wedding ball
a lost Hasid—like a Messiah—stands by the wall
blocking with his body the graffiti *"Vanya and Vasya were here"*

O Brooklyn of Orthodox churches synagogues and mosques
O Brooklyn of the Chinese and Hindus—a disciple and a teacher
the tearoom proprietor—it seems—lost his patience
mockingly—he says—*right now I close*

і вимикає світло — що ж він на те є бос
з кухні виходять дружина двійко дітей і пес

я затискаю серветку наче кронштейном парус
як завжди підступна самотність приходить із віршем на пару
як завжди скриплять яхти — наче рубанком столяр —
і чайок вночі похитує важка тканина води
вдихаю солярки запах який мені зносить дим
чомусь в зеленому світлі як випраний долар

бруклин це ломаний шеляг або поржавілий крейцер
світло нічного потягу що мчить по сталевій рейці
і його наздогнати не можна — спіймати також не мож
він залишається в тобі *ванею зіною педро*
чайками над коні айленд — кирилицею напевно
котра на серветці схожа на посірілий мох

<2011>

and turns off the lights—after all he's the boss
his wife two kids and a dog come out of the kitchen

I squeeze the napkin like a sail with a bracket
as always wily loneliness and verse come paired
as always the yachts creak—like a carpenter's drawknife
and the heavy fabric of water rocks the seagulls at night
I inhale the smell of diesel fuel brought down to me by smoke
which shimmers in the green light like a washed dollar bill

Brooklyn is like a broken farthing or a rusty penny
like the light of a night train speeding on a steel rail
and it's impossible to overtake it—or to catch it
Brooklyn abides within you as *Vanya Zina Pedro*
as the seagulls on Coney island—as the Cyrillic writing
which on the napkin surely looks like grayish moss

<2011>

Translated by Orest Popovych

Бруклінська елегія

щоранку пекарні єврейські відчиняють з пітьми
перше що добігає — схожий на прудкість лисиць —
запах цинамону — розтертих із цукром яєць —
до цегляних синагог — і це є початком зими
бо тісто пахне сосною і зірваний вчора жасмин
разом із часником і цибулею сиґналить тобі з полиць

од сьомої починається лящання металевих замків
іржання сабвею — перегуки вуличних продавців —
вантажники носять фрукти залежно від попиту й цін
і кавуни смугасті схожі на тигрів з боків
а гарбузи галувинські — на голівудських дів
вантажники мексиканці — на олімпійських борців

а школярі підскакують: ось — жовтий шкільний автобус
стара підмітає вулицю — смердить дешевий тютюн
бруклін вовтузиться зранку — скаржачись на самоту
на драконячу ненажерливість і на свою хворобу
на металевий міст, що вигнувся наче хобот
на це муравлище люду що знищить колись сатурн

хасиди — мов чорна смородина — обліпили гілля синагог
вони виноград арамейський — уманська глина і клей
дратва якою зшиває темні слова юдей
накинувши талес на голову — йому щось шепоче бог
і діти його щебечуть — мов райські пташки — бо
виспівує йому бруклін хлібом і рипом дверей

кожним коліном юдейським — рядком що теплий як сир
геометрією кабали — камінням єрусалиму
співом жінок в пекарні які наковтались диму
калаталом перед суботою — і молоком від кози
християнин — до пекарні; до синагоги — хасид
і — зголоднівши бруклін — ковтає слину

<2011>

Brooklyn Elegy

each morning the Jewish bakeries open up out of the darkness
first to reach the brick synagogues—with the swiftness of foxes—
is the scent of cinnamon—eggs beaten with sugar—
and this is how winters begin
for the dough smells of pine and the freshly picked jasmine
blended with garlic and onions beckons to you from the shelves

at seven starts the clanging of metal locks
the screeching of the subway—the shouting of street vendors—
they unload fruit according to demand and prices
striped melons that look like tigers on their sides
Halloween pumpkins—like Hollywood dames
the Mexican unloaders—like Olympic wrestlers

school children jump up and down—their yellow school bus is here
an old woman sweeps the street—the stench of cheap tobacco fills the air
Brooklyn bustles in the morning—griping about being forlorn
about the draconic greediness and its own ailment
about the metal bridge arching like the trunk of an elephant
about this human ant hill that some day will be sacked by Saturn

the Hasids—like black currants—have covered the branches of the synagogues
they're the Aramaic grapes—the clay and glue of Uman
the shoemaker's thread used to stitch together obscure words by a Hebrew man
with a tallith on his head—God whispers to him His advice—
and his children chirp—like birds of paradise—
Brooklyn sings to him with bread and the creaking of doors

with every Hebrew generation—each line of print as warm as cheese
with the geometry of the cabala—with the stones of Jerusalem
with the song of the women in the bakery who've inhaled enough smoke
with a clapper rattling before the sabbath—and the milk of a goat
a Christian—heads to a bakery; a Hasid—to a synagogue
and—Brooklyn feeling hungry—swallows its saliva

<2011>

Translated by Orest Popovych

Staten Island

Статен Айленд — це острів це значить — каліка на милицях
Пором допливе — GPS не помилиться
І вздовж океану бейсбольні поля й Каподано
бульвар — де самотньо і вітряно — грудень і січень
Цей острів що сам собі простір позичив
з крамницями і рестораном

дійде аж по котики в зимну Атлантику — Значить
він ключ що заводить «Тойоту» — Він бачить
і міст Verrazano і обриси бруклінських вилиць
і кульчик у вусі — ну по приколу цей пірсинґ —
і ще кораблі — що пливуть до Нью-Джерзі
обмерзлі в снігах — що прийшли і звалились —

засипавши пагорби й вулички — музейного Будду
припарковану «Alfa Romeo» — номер якої забуду
поле для гольфу — старих італійців з футболом
з піцою й фільмами про незнищенність мафії
п'ють у траторіях каву — їдять шоколадний muffin
їх сицилійський захист продірявлено голом

насправді на Статен Айленді тиша зсувається снігом
забивається мишею в темінь — сірим білчиним бігом
пахне китайським супом та італійським тістом
скупченням чорних ліктів і баскетбольних майок
джазом погоні за автом яке в опівніч зникає
від поліцейських «Chevy» — в хроніці завтра помістять

мені ця зима в снігопадах диктує листи і вірші
прогулянки вздовж океану якими нічого не вирішиш
тому що писання книги це споглядання руху
це підглядання в шпарку дверного замка — й собача
пристрасть обнюхати простір — і біля пірсу побачити
пару котра цілується тримаючись міцно за руки

тому що життя за сорок каже дивитись простіше:
і не питатись для чого порівну снігу і тиші
і ще також не питатись — що означають знаки
й чому в цих снігах твій сумнів — неначе сліпці наосліп —

Staten Island

Staten Island—is an island meaning—a cripple on crutches
a ferry will get you there—the GPS won't miss it
and along the ocean baseball fields and Capodano
boulevard—desolate and windy—in December and January
This island which has borrowed the space it needs
with shops and restaurants

will immerse up to its ankles into the frigid Atlantic—Meaning
it is the key that starts a Toyota—It views
both the Verrazano bridge and the outlines of Brooklyn's jaw bones
and sees an earring—this ear piercing as a challenge
and then the ships—which sail to New Jersey
iced up from the snows—that came down heavily

burying hillocks and streets—and the Buddha at the museum
a parked Alfa Romeo—whose number I'll forget
a golf course—and the old Italians enjoying soccer
pizza and films about an indestructible mafia
drinking coffee in trattorias—eating chocolate muffins
their Sicilian defense penetrated by a goal

In reality on Staten Island stillness is displaced by the sliding snow
it scurries like a mouse into darkness—darting like a gray squirrel
there's the smell of Chinese soup and Italian dough
the gathering of black elbows and basketball shirts
the jazzy chase of a car which at midnight eludes
police Chevys—and will make tomorrow's paper

to me this winter with its snowfalls dictates letters and verses
walks along the ocean that will resolve nothing
because writing a book is like observing motion
like peeping through a lock in the door—and the canine
passion to sniff all around your space—and by the pier to spy
on a couple kissing while firmly holding hands

because life after forty tells you to look at things more simply:
and not to ask why snow and stillness come in equal parts
and also not to ask about the meaning of signs
and why in these snows your doubts—feeling their way like blind people—

суне тобі на зустріч — і пахне пташиний послід
бо все це — братан — ти мусив й до того знати

тому-то цей острів пригрівши припарковану «Alfa Romeo»
на яку повсідалися птахи переважно надуті меви
ділиться снігом і словом — як сиґаретами — кент
і каже тобі не питати про принцип життя і пропорцій
і птахам зимовим що гріються в теплій протоці
ти кидаєш хліб з розгону — і вслід випадковий цент

<2011>

are pushing towards you—there's the stench of bird droppings
for all of this—bro—you must have known before

therefore this island having warmed up the parked Alfa Romeo
with birds sitting on it mainly puffed up seagulls
is sharing with you the snow and the word—like cigarettes—a friend
and tells you not to question life's principles and proportions
and to the winter birds warming themselves on the strait
you toss some bread on the run—followed by an occasional cent

<2011>

Translated by Orest Popovych

Мар'яна Савка

Одинадцята-стріт

сняться сни
в них крізь мене проходять мости
їхні вигнуті хорди
прохромлюють серце й аорти
і випирають крізь ребра
манхеттен з бродвеєм
чорні тунелі сабвеїв
і до нудоти чітка геометрія вулиць
одинадцята-стріт
має ж мати яку-небудь пам'ять про мене
може відбиток мого обцаса
в розм'яклім асфальті
з того часу коли
я ув'язнула в літі у місті у миті
а проте це не надто важливо
лишіть мені скибку
зачерствілого чорного хліба
годувати на осінь старих голубів
руками блакитно-прозорими
без жодного натяку
на свою приналежність
до шляхетної раси
яка там шляхетність
я не вмію іще говорити до них
голубиною мовою
вмію лишень
губи кусати надсадно
до крові
очевидно ж
з любові

<2008>

Maryana Savka

Eleventh Street

I have dreams
in which bridges pass through me
their curved chords
pierce my heart and aorta
and protrude from between my ribs
Manhattan and Broadway
the black tunnels of the subway and
the sickeningly precise geometry of streets
eleventh street
should have some memory of me
maybe an imprint of my high heel
in the softened asphalt
from the time
I got stuck in the city for a moment one summer
though, it's not that important
leave me a slice of
stale black bread
to feed the old pigeons in fall
from my transparent blue hands
with no hint
of my belonging to an
aristocratic race
what aristocracy do you mean
I still don't know how to talk to them
in the language of pigeons
I only know how
to bite my lips
until they bleed
out of love
of course

<2008>

Translated by Ostap Kin and Ali Kinsella

Оксана Луцишина

* * *

Мій друг Стефан у вельветовому піджаку фотографується
з різними жінками які купують його книжки
він сяє усмішкою і так само сяють ці жінки, що запопали його на маленьку
    вічність.
Я сиджу у кав'ярні над своїми нотатками і плачу. Моя дочка
зоставалася у мене на вихідні, вона така велика і незалежна,
а я і досі не знаю, яке материнство на смак.

Моя подруга Діана лежить у ліжку і дивиться серіал про Декстера, час від
    часу
повертаючись до завдання з лінгвістики, і питає у мене: рідна мова —
що це для тебе? — і я відказую:
це дім, у якому немає місця для темряви.

Портланд і Тампа і Нью-Йорк і всі інші міста, малі і великі — це контейнери
із повітрям, повним минулого, це запечатані Едеми пам'яті.
Сьогодні вночі мені снилося, що я вивчила фізику і хімію і ще безліч усяких
    наук,
і тепер знаю все що лише можна знати про кожен атом
вони танцюють мені перед очима і я пояснюю кожен із їхніх рухів котримось
    із законів світобудови,

Але, знаючи все, так і не можу перестати вірити в Бога.

2014

Oksana Lutsyshyna

* * *

My friend Stefan in the corduroy jacket is taking selfies
with the various women who are buying his book
he's all smiles and so are they, happy to have caught him for a short eternity.
I am going over my notes in a coffee shop and crying. My daughter
stayed with me over the weekend; she is so big and independent,
yet I still have no idea what motherhood tastes like.

My roommate Diana is lying on her bed watching *Dexter*, from time to time
returning to her linguistics homework. She asks me, "*native language*,
what's it for you?" and I answer,
"It's a house with no room for darkness."

Portland and Tampa and New York and all other cities big and little are but
containers of air filled with the past, those sealed Edens of memory.
Last night I dreamt I learned physics and chemistry and all the other sciences
and now I know all there is to know about every atom
they dance before my eyes and I explain each of their movements with
some law of the universe,

But, knowing everything, I cannot stop believing in god.

2014

Translated by the author and Ali Kinsella

Катерина Бабкіна

Знеболювальне і снодійне

З міста, котре ніколи не дає тобі спати,
пестить тебе так солодко, чавить так безнадійно —
друзі просили різне: соуси, фотоапарати,
косметику і якусь мозаїку пиздувату,
телефони, насіння, кеди. І тільки Катя
попросила знеболювальне й снодійне.
Господи, проведи нас в Бруклін без джипіеса,
перепиши нам візи з кончених на постійні.
Я би здала їй всіх борделів і барів адреси,
я привезла б їй чайку чи чорношкіру принцесу —
але вона просила знеболювальне й снодійне.
Всі трудові мігранти, бляді, стипендіати,
менеджери і няньки, бабки діаспорійні,
всі, хто сюди дістався в радості помирати —
потерпають від болю, моляться на ніч матом,
запивають знеболювальне, марячи про снодійне.
Катя, над океаном ніч заплутує сіті,
на найдальшому стріті, в найбруднішому барі
нудить іще до того, як замовив і випив.
Всім нам болить так само — тобі і мені, і дітям
рибалок із Чайна-тауну, котрі не сплять, щоб ловити
свіжі морепродукти для досвітніх базарів.

2014

Kateryna Babkina

Painkillers and Sleeping Pills

From the city that never lets you sleep,
which caresses so sweetly and presses so harshly,
friends asked for so many different things: sauces, cameras,
cosmetics, some fucking mosaic,
telephones, seeds, Keds. But Katya
asked for painkillers and sleeping pills.
Lord, lead us into Brooklyn without our GPS,
change our visas from temporary to permanent.
I would give her the addresses of all the bordellos and bars;
I'd bring her a seagull or even a dusky princess,
but she wanted painkillers and sleeping pills.
All the migrant workers, whores, and scholarship students,
managers, nannies, and diaspora grannies
who came here to die happy,
suffer from pains, and curse through their prayers at night,
take painkillers, and dream about sleeping pills.
Katya, night tangles the nets in the ocean,
it nauseates you before you order and drink
on the farthest street in the dirtiest bar.
We all hurt the same—you, me, and the kids
of the Chinatown fishermen, who don't sleep
to catch the freshest seafood for the markets at dawn.

2014

Translated by Virlana Tkacz and Wanda Phipps

Ірина Шувалова

велика риба та інші мости

1

учора містом ходила велика риба
я знаю я сам це бачив я саме міряв
на себе вулицю як затісну сорочку
або незнайому жінку. тоді розверзся
автобус, і я пройшов через дим людей
дерева тремтіли задерши спідниці. ноги
зануривши голі в холодні озера вітрин
із неба цідилося біле сумне молоко
коли я спинився скрутити собі папіросу
смішні мої пальці комизились наче граблі
гіркий мій язик наче п'яний заточувавсь в роті
коли я спитався у тебе куди мені йти
планета хитнулась — і ти показала на захід
як порожньо стало у світі як довго я спав
дивися відколи я їв всі хліби скам'яніли
відколи я пив захлинулась собою вода
і полум'я згасло
вона засміялась «це ж ніч
вночі в цьому місті трапляються речі які
при світлі нагадують янголів з білого сиру
а в темряві носять навиворіт лиця — і так
збивають зі сліду криваву ліхтарну армаду»
вона б говорила іще але риба пройшла
повз нас обережно гойдаючи мужнім хвостом
аби не збудити заснулого поруч безхатька
в його непорочному коконі жовтих газет
вона завернула за ріг на cathedral і broadway
ми тіні сховали в кишені і сіли в метро

Iryna Shuvalova

big fish and other bridges

1.
yesterday a big fish walked through the city
I know I saw it myself I was just trying on
the street like a tight shirt
or a strange woman. then a bus erupted
and I walked through the smoke of people
the trees trembled hiking up their skirts. naked
legs sunk into the the window display's cold lakes
gloomy white milk seeped down from the sky
when I stopped to roll myself a cigarette
my comical fingers moved like rakes
my bitter tongue staggered in my mouth as if drunk
when I asked you where I should go
the planet swayed—and you pointed west
how empty the world became how long have I slept
look since I last ate bread has turned to stone
since I last drank the water has choked on itself
and the flames went out
she laughed "but it's night
at night things happen in this city which
in the light resemble angels made from white cheese
but in the dark they wear their faces inside out—and thus
evade detection by the bloody armada of streetlights"
she would have explained more but the fish walked
by us cautiously swinging its formidable tale
so as not to wake the homeless guy nearby
in his immaculate cocoon of yellowed papers
she turned on the corner of cathedral and broadway
we hid the shadows in our pockets and got on the subway

2

ти розгойдуєшся — й переступаєш поріг
виносиш себе за двері
на довгих ношах горизонтального вітру
кімната чіпляється за тебе каже не йди не йди
ну та як не йди

коли літо скінчилось а по ньому не сталось нічого
коли місто розбилось об сірий брезентовий берег
і загрузло по вікна й навіки лишилося тут

я не знаю чи ти помітив але відколи дні
почали коротшати я не знаю коли це було торік?
може давніше я не пригадую фішка в тому
що вони коротшають і досі що жодна весна
жодне літо не здатне запобігти скручуванню пружинки
тіла старіють світила гаснуть скисає в холодильнику молоко

ми
так далеко від усього коли сидимо на парапеті
коли повз нас пропливають жовті слова машини
повітря саксофон бігун голуб подружжя
геїв слова запах бургерів печаль зрештою дощ
ми так далеко
наші дні коротшають

і коли ти виходиш вночі покурити на сходах
у будинку всі сплять тільки пральна машинка не спить
якщо очі заплющити можна підслухати шелест
це ворушиться час як велика підземна ріка

2.

gathering momentum—you cross the threshold
carry yourself through the doorway
on the wind's long horizontal stretcher
the room entreats you don't go don't go
but how can you not go

after summer was over nothing happened
when the city shattered against the gray canvas shore
and sunk up to its windows and stayed so forever

I don't know if you noticed but since the days
started to get shorter I don't know when that was last year?
maybe earlier I don't remember the thing is
they are getting shorter still and up to now not a single spring
not a single summer has ever been able to prevent the spring from coiling
bodies age heavenly lights fade milk sours in the fridge

we
are so distant from everything as we sit on the railing
as past us flow yellow words cars
the wind a saxophone a jogger a pigeon a gay
couple the smell of burgers sadness finally rain
we are so far away
our days are getting shorter

and when you go out at night to have a smoke on the stairs
everyone in the building is asleep only the washing machine doesn't sleep
if you close your eyes you can hear the rustling
it's time moving like a giant underground river

3

із чого складається місто?
із пари
із вуст
із парків де сплять волоцюги, із теплих квартир
де вікна впускають крізь штори оголений ранок
із псів що здебільшого майже не гидять публічно
метро що везе нас мостами в ранковий туман
коли ми вертаємось з віліджа в іншу країну
де сонні жінки не знаходять у сумці ключів
дрімають на ґанках у комір сховавши лице
із протягів що обіймають крізь куртки і пальта
із вицвілих фото в старих антикварних крамничках
іще не знайомих сухих нікотинових губ
лакованих і елегантних печальних індійців
які випливають із чорних своїх колісниць
давай по капкейку а потім поромом на айленд
коли я питаю як вийти на твенті ван іст
мені посміхаються жалісно як ідіотці
дивись яка класна татуха який падолист
загублений шалик вже тиждень живе на паркані
сусід виїжджав би на джоб чи не першим метром
однак що робити коли воно цілодобове
а інший сусід ще не спить стереже свою тінь
тут фрідом і ліберті разом як з діром аскольд
як джонсон із джонсоном. меланхолійно в підземці
викручує ґвинтики з радості віолончель
якщо підійти зовсім близько до краю в тумані
окреслиться міст ворухнеться велика вода
бігун кашляне шелеснувши крилатим кросівком
невидима тінь — ну і я тут невидима тінь
стою мовчазна носаком колупаючи пам'ять
якщо я тебе оближу язиком океану
вві сні — чи проснувшися будеш любити мене?

3.

what is the city made from?
from steam
from mouths
from parks where vagrants sleep, from warm apartments
where windows let the naked morning seep in through the shades
and dogs that for the most part don't shit in public
the subway that carries us over bridges in the morning fog
when we are coming back from a Village into another country
where tired women are fumbling for keys in their bags
they doze on porches hiding their faces in their collars
from gusts that embrace through jackets and coats
from faded photos in old antiquarian shops
yet unfamiliar dry nicotine lips
from lacquered and elegant sad Indians
who stream out of their black chariots
let's have a cupcake and then take the ferry to the Island
when I ask how to find east 21st
they smile at me awkwardly like I'm an idiot
look at that cool tattoo what an autumn
a lost scarf has been living on the fence for a week now
our neighbor would be taking the very first subway to work
but that's not an option in the city where it runs around the clock
your choice doesn't matter when it runs 24 hours a day
and the other neighbor isn't asleep he is guarding his shadow
here freedom and liberty go together like Dir and Askold
or Johnson and Johnson. with melancholy in the subway
the cello is unscrewing the pegs out of happiness
if you walk to the very edge in the fog
the bridge becomes visible the big water stirs
the runner coughs his winged sneakers squeak
an invisible shadow—and so am I
I stand silent kicking up memory with my shoe
if I lick you with an ocean's tongue
in a dream—when you awaken will you love me?

4
якщо вийти за двері
замкнути в квартирі ключі перейти одразу
дорогу в недозволеному місці викинути
обгортку від льодяника в смітник проминути
перехрестя не вітатися ні з ким навіть
зі знайомим барменом що вийшов на перекур
пройти два квартали потім наприклад
ще два але в іншому
напрямку скористатися транспортним засобом
вийти на незнайомій зупинці
зникнути

імовірно ніхто так і не згадає що ми жили тут
що наші вікна виходили на великий будинок з рекламним білбордом
і баром на першому поверсі (привіт бармен)
ніхто не знатиме
як лежачи ночами в ліжку ми довго
дивились на стелю повну відбитків світла
думали про літо роботу вибори ні про що конкретно про нас
засинаючи слухали
шелест великої ріки

2015

4.

if we were to walk out the door
lock our keys in the apartment then immediately
jay-walk across the street throw out
the wrapper from the popsicle in the garbage pass through
an intersection not greeting anyone not even
our buddy the bartender who came out for a smoke
walk two blocks and then for example
walk two more but walk in another
direction use public transportation
get out at an unfamiliar stop
disappear

it's likely that no one would ever remember that we lived here
that our windows looked out on a big building with billboards
with the bar on the first floor (hi bartender)
no one would know
how at night lying in bed we stared
at the ceiling full of imprints of light for a long time
thinking about summer work elections nothing in particular us
how falling asleep we listened
to the whisper of the great river

2015

Translated by Olena Jennings

Ірина Вікирчак

Р.А.

Розо,
ти знала
як почути бога у самому серці мангеттену
якимось чином ловила руками
алюмінієві спіралі пружин
що звисають з неба

а потім відходила на безпечну відстань
до єдиної яблуні
в центральному парку
і вибирала слова
закладала їх в яблуко замість зерен
і відправляла пружиною в космос
відпускала

Розо,
я знаю, ти чула
голоси поколінь, що застрягли в повітрі
між тридцять четвертою й п'ятою авеню
сортувала їх по зайнятих офісах
телефонних кабелях і телеграфу до європи

а також в радіоефіри нью-йоркських служб таксі
і водії, бадьорі і байдужі
приймали їхні замовлення
їхали за неіснуючими адресами
блукали
зникали
звільняли

2015

Iryna Vikyrchak

To R. A.

Rose,
you knew
how to find God in the very heart of Manhattan
your hands could somehow catch
the aluminum spirals of springs
that hang down from the sky.

and then you'd withdraw to a safe distance,
to the only apple tree
in Central Park
and you'd select words,
put them into an apple instead of seeds
and use the springs to send them out into space
you let them go

Rose,
I knew you heard
the voices of the generations that got stuck in the air
between Thirty-Fourth Street and Fifth Avenue
you sorted them among busy offices
telephone cables and telegraphs to Europe

as well as on the New York taxi cab frequency
and the drivers, cheerful and indifferent,
accepted their dispatches
drove toward nonexistent addresses
wandered
vanished
liberated

2015

Translated by Ostap Kin and Ali Kinsella

Сезонна

Autumn cannot bereave us.
Rose Ausländer

Щоби пізнати Господа —
і ти про це думаєш
кожного разу на злітній смузі, —
треба вдивлятися у далекі вогні,
пам'ятати про гравітацію,
вивчати фізику.

Робити знімки перехожим,
заглядати їм в очі і душу.
Кожні півроку переїжджати,
аби набирати повітря в легені,
винирнувши.

Щоб подолати сезонну, —
глядіти в обличчя страхам,
покладатись на психосоматику,
думати про смерть і змиритись,
з її неминучістю чи пізніше,
чи вже сьогодні.

Втікати, щоб не згубитись,
чекати посадки потойбік,
де любов продається
в книгарнях й Старбаксі.
Приймати, не роздивившись,
порушивши вивчену фізику,
як аксіому сезонну:
що кожної осені
кожного
з нас
є потрохи
в Нью-Йорку,
і трохи
Нью-Йорку
у кожному
з нас.

2015

Seasonal

> *Autumn cannot bereave us.*
> *Rose Ausländer*

In order to understand God—
and this is something you think about
every time you're on a runway—
you need to stare into distant lights,
remember gravity,
and study physics.
Take snapshots for passersby,
look into their eyes and souls.
Move every six months
so you can fill your lungs with air
when you emerge onto the surface.
In order to overcome the seasonal,
stare your fears in the face,
rely on psychosomatic medicine,
think about death and come to terms with
its inevitability—either later
or even today.
Run away so you don't get lost,
await your landing on the other side
where love is sold
in bookstores and Starbucks.
Accept without question,
ignoring what you learned in physics,
like a seasonal axiom:
that every fall
there's a little bit
of each
of us
in New York,
and a little bit
of New York
in each
of us.

2015

Translated by Ostap Kin and Ali Kinsella

Олександр Фразе-Фразенко

в Maikley

але якось виходить так, що тема кожного мого фільму завжди мусить зникати.
вона мусить вивітрюватися, вона, як Paradise Lost Джона Мільтона, вона
     втрата.
і саме зникання, як сюжетну обставину, тепер маю не вперше. Чубай втрачає
щільність тіла, зникаючи серед лісу, хоч спершись на дерево — повертається.
тепер я змусив Махна зникати в аеропорту Chicago O'Hare, відлітають літаки
і забирають стіни його дому з собою, і той дім на сімох вітрах. неділя пополудні,
мій мозок наповнений мухами. хочу зустрітися зі своєю дівчиною, коли приїду.

Марко не може знайти фотографію, де Лишега танцює на його весіллі. я
     не можу
знайти книжки з мого дитинства, не можу знайти Калинцевого Пана Ніхта.
     чи це
означає, що — так, я теж є ним, тобто Ніхтом, приміряю його невидимий
     костюм.
мої фільми ж тільки про мене, тож глядач нехай займається своїми справами,
     а я
своїми. риба з базару запливає в моє вікно зі своїм запахом. на собі бачу темне
комфортне місце, куди вона запливає. можу піти за нею, як пес, входжу ж туди,
ніби ключ. тобто, я не хочу роздумувати над цим, просто збираюся переповідати
сюжет, схожий на втрату й повернення раю. але сьогодні я, як і сотні моїх сестер
змучений від диму без вогню, хоча сьогодні добрий день, не зважаючи на дим.
сьогодні не існує моєї любові, тихий пісок обирає мої пальці сьогодні,
     сьогодні ти
вся в квітах, одною з германських мов проведена ця ламана лінія, я вимірюю ці
два місяці зеленим спокоєм вітру навесні, тоді й Фредерік Лов Олмстед вписав
мій силует в ці зелені овали і під ці овальні мости, давно запланована комбінація.

Oleksandr Fraze-Frazenko

At Maikley's Café

and it turns out to be so that the theme of my every film is like John Milton's
Paradise Lost, it must evaporate, it is as though it must disappear, it is a loss.
now, the disappearance as a plot device, I have done that before. Chubay lost
his body, vanishing in the woods—though, leaning onto a tree, he returned.
then I forced Makhno to disappear at the Chicago's O'Hare airport, planes
    departed
and took walls of his house with them, that house on seven winds. Sunday
    afternoon,
my brain is full of flies. I want to see my girl when I arrive.

Marko could not find the photo where Lysheha dances at his wedding. I cannot
find a book from my childhood, I cannot find Kalynet's Mr. Nobody. does that
mean that I am also him, meaning Nobody? I am trying on his invisible costume.
my films are about me and the viewers can simply mind their own business, and I
shall mind mine. a fish from the market swims through my window, with its
    stench. I see
a dark cozy place where it swims. I can follow its fins, like a dog; I enter there
as a key. I mean, I don't want to think about it, I am simply trying to tell the plot.
looks like an prodigious failure and paradise is found. but today I am, like my
    sisters' fleet,
weary of smoke without fire, although today is a good day, despite the smoke.

today my love does not exist, quiet sand pricks my fingers today, today you are
full of flowers; a Germanic language drew this broken line, I divide these
months in two with the green tranquility of the wind in spring, Frederick Law
    Olmsted wrote
my silhouette into green ovals and under these oval bridges a well-planned
    combination.
but I go further, the quagmire swallows me and then spits, so today I am
in Chinatown, Brooklyn, on the corner of Fifty-Ninth Street and Eighth Avenue
at the Maikley Cafe, and three blocks away the Chinese showed up here, here
    they
came out of deep earth, digging a hole in their Tulou, until they saw lights

але йду далі, трясовина повинна мене ковтати й випльовувати тож сьогодні я

сиджу в Chinatown Brooklyn на розі п'ятдесят дев'ятої вулиці та восьмої
авеню

в Maikley Cafe, і до речі, трьома блоками нижче китайці взялися тут, тут
вони й

вийшли з глибини землі, копавши діру в своєму тулоу, аж поки побачили
світло

крізь двері супермаркету. мене впізнає красива китаянка, певно з Фуцзянь
(був її дід),

музики нема. якби я сидів не сам, навряд писав би вірш. але ось я виходжу

з будинку, ось відчиняю двері, ось я сиджу перед вікном і китайці дивляться на

мене, як на захід, в якого широко відкриті очі, і не бачать мене. наша зустріч має

ознаку випадковості, наша зустріч має запах солі й луску, я привіз для тебе
кашель

із заходу, цей Brooklyn позначений слизом моїх бронхів, такий слід слимака, але

такі слимаки не мали б жити на цьому континенті, принаймні це ознака виду. не

можу знайти Пана Ніхта, бо його й не було ніколи. думаю, пишу вірші,
так думаю.

на світлих лісових узліссях має бути дім слимака. з іншого боку, мій   улюблений

режисер гей, мій улюблений вірш написав потопельник. що я маю робити з цим.

там щодня сходить сонце, на те він і схід, на заході ми теж таке маємо.
дивно, але

виходить так, що кожен мій фільм позначений слизом моїх бронхів і це
може стати

хронічним захворюванням. я надіюся на китайську зупу з креветками й
морськими

кониками, а також на її тепло. зігрій мене, дозволь відхаркувати, дозволь
бути

поетом у Нью-Йорку, дозволь ходити стежками, які перехрещуються,
дозволь

бути хлопчиком, який має пластикового морського коника і бавиться ним
у воді,

дозволь ковтати твоє тепло, бо кожний поет у Нью-Йорку хоче бути
поетом у Нью-

Йорку. ще так далеко до неї, ще так близько до неї, так близько до тебе,
музики

нема. я називаю це поезією, думайте так зі мною на світлих узліссях лісу
навесні.

2015

through the door of a supermarket. a beautiful Chinese girl recognizes me, probably out of Fujian (was her ancestor), no music here. if I wasn't alone I would less likely write a poem. I exit
the building, I open the door, here I am facing the window and the Chinese are looking at
me as if I was the West with wide open eyes, but they do not see. our meeting has all
signs of chance, it has a smell of salt and fish scales, I brought this cough for you
from the West, this Brooklyn is marked with mucus of bronchi, like a snail trail, but
such snails should not live on this continent, at least this is a species' sign. I
cannot find Mr. Nobody because he never existed. I think; I write poetry, so I think.

at the light-filled forest edges there should be a snail house. on the other hand, my favorite
director is gay, the poet who wrote my favorite poem drowned. what should I do with this?
there every day the sun rises, it is east after all, in the west we also have that. amazingly, but
without cessation my every film is marked with mucus from my bronchi and it may become a
chronic disease. I have hopes for this Chinese soup with shrimp and seahorses, I have hope for her warmth. warm me up, allow me to expectorate, let me be
a poet in New York, allow me to walk paths that intersect, let me
be a boy who has a plastic seahorse and who plays in the water with it,
let me swallow your warmth, for each poet in New York wants to be a poet in New York. still she is so far, still she is so close, you are so close, the music
is not. this is poetry, think just like me in the bright edges of forests in spring.

2015

Translated by Olga Gerasymiv

Василь Лозинський

Нью-Йорк

Колода в оці — великий хмародер.
Немає кому сказати, що недобре
так, якщо щось втрапляє
в око з хмародера.
Піщинка в оці — не колода.

2015

Vasyl Lozynsky

New York

The beam in my eye is a huge skyscraper,
there is no one to tell how awful it is
when something lands in
your eye from a skyscraper.
The grain of sand in my eye is not a beam.

2015

Translated by Ostap Kin and Ali Kinsella

Юлія Мусаковська

* * *

Тунелями білого кахлю курсують жовті рибини,
всі на одну подобу, але з різними голосами.
Цей острів знає всі їхні мови. Довкола спінене,
море їхнім пісням підспівує безперестанно.
Мистецтво співіснувати з несхожими у довірі,
без втрати себе. Острів забув, що було інакше.
Тунелі, схожі на довгі сурми, протяжно виючи,
тримають його, мов корабель тримають канати.
Щось мусить тримати, коли навколо стільки свободи.
Щось мусить не дати тобі загубити напрям.
Коли у графіті в метро проступить обличчя Бога,
разом зацвітуть абрикос, тюльпани і сакура.

І ти сорок піших кварталів до Сентрал-парку
летиш, перемішаний диханням із юрбою,
де в кожного в цьому потоці — в окремій парості —
занадто багато страшної спорідненості з тобою.
У клерка в новому взутті, начищеному до мігрені,
у вірменина, що лається за кермом супер-шатла,
у матері з немовлям, у гіпі з флягою на ремені,
у азіатки-студентки з химерно накрученим шарфом.

Навіщо тобі це гірке й надкушене яблуко світу,
обурливі погляди класиків у спорожнілих алеях,
ця спроба ловитвою вітру себе зцілити,
коли повітряну кулю прошили шпилі сталеві.
Стрибнути з верхівки Емпайр-Стейту у порожнечу
струною за пояс обв'язаний, наче напнутим нервом.
І аж унизу здивуватись: як стрімко і безкінечно
пожежні драбини червоних будинків ростуть у небо.

2016

Yulia Musakovska

* * *

Yellow fish course through white-tiled tunnels
all bear the same faces, but have different voices.
This isle knows all of their sounds. In foam all around
the sea sings along to their songs without ceasing.
The art of coexisting with strangers: still trusting
without losing the self. The isle forgot there is any other way.
The tunnels are like trumpets that howl
they hold the isle as ropes hold a vessel.
Something must moor it against so much freedom.
Something must keep straight your course.
When the image of God is traced in subway graffiti,
Apricots, sakura, tulips together will blossom.

And you fly forty blocks to Central Park
mixed with the breath of this crowd,
where everyone in this flow—in a separate shoot—
holds too much dreadful affinity with you:
A clerk in new shoes, shined superbly;
An Armenian cussing, driving his SuperShuttle;
A mother with child; a hippie with a hip flask;
An Asian student with a scarf strangely wrapped covering her neck.

Why do you need this bitter and bitten Big Apple,
the outrageous look of the classics in empty alleys,
this attempt to heal yourself by catching wind,
when the hot-air balloon is pierced with steel spires.
Dive off the top of Empire State into the void,
tied by the belt with a string, like a pulled nerve.
At the bottom, however, you will be overjoyed
Seeing buildings, red ladders of fire, sprout up with verve.

2016

Translated by Olga Gerasymiv and Jazlyn Kraft

Ольга Фразе-Фразенко

Грудень

В аеропорті єврейські діти з капелюшними пуделками.
Ми наближаємось до брами. Жінка в шалику
з американським прапором і надписом Love на ґумці
лосинів з нами полетить за океан. В літаку зустрічаю Вірляну,
яка каже, що світ тісний. Ми плутаємо гілки метро та напрямки:
Лорімер стейшн і там, і тут. Виходимо з підземелля.
Чіпляємось з картою до людей. Ти питаєш, чи я відчуваю повітря.
Кажу: ні, я просто втомилась і хочу спати.
За кілька днів ми підемо пішки від Фултон до Фултон
дерев'яним мостом в такому світлі, яке люблю, в такому,
аби було видно острів і лінію, якою ходить фері.
Аби було тісно і велосипедисти вели ровери у руках.
Аби я клацала це все на плівку. І закоханих на мості клацала
на телефон, щоби викладати на фейсбук: мовляв, ось подивіться:
любов є, вона є, прямо тут на Бруклінському мості.
У нічному пабі Монро теж є любов, але вже інша.
Я нічого не знаю про це. Я тримаюсь осторонь.
Я купую дурнувату шапку і кольорові штани.
Я заходжу у Старбакс зловити вайфай, надсилаю фото,
Він питає: де ти є, ти в безпеці, коли повернешся?
Маленькі песики дивляться із вітрини, б'ють лапками,
Кажуть: купи, купи. Я шукаю ознаки дому або знаки,
які туди приведуть. Шукаю вуличну піцу і зелену кулю сабвею.
Садівники міста садять декоративну капусту навколо дерев.
Місто вбирають, як новорічну ялинку.

2016

Olha Fraze-Frazenko

December

At the airport, Jewish kids are carrying their hatboxes.
We approach our gate. A woman wearing an American-flag scarf
and stretchy leggings with the word *Love* on them will fly across the ocean
with us. On the plane I run into Virlana who says the world is
small. We get the subway lines and directions confused:
Lorimer Station is both here and there. We come up out of the subway.
We're bothering people with our map. You ask if I feel the air.
I say: no, I'm just tired and I want to sleep.
In a few days we'll walk from Fulton Station to Fulton Station
across the wooden bridge and in that light that I like, the kind
where you can see the island and the ferry's path.
Where it's packed and cyclists have to walk their bikes.
Where I capture it all on film. And I use my phone to take pictures
of couples to post on Facebook, so that I can say, look:
love is real, here it is right on the Brooklyn Bridge.
Love is also the Monro Pub at night, but it is different.
I don't know anything about that one. I stay away from it.
I buy a silly hat and colorful pants.
I enter a Starbucks looking for wi-fi, I send photos.
He asks: where are you, are you safe, when are you coming back?
Tiny puppies stare out from windows they hit with their paws.
They're saying: buy us, buy us. I look for indications of home or signs
that will lead me there. I look for dollar slices and the green globe of the subway.
The city's gardeners plant decorative cabbages around the trees.
The city is being trimmed like a Christmas tree.

2016

Translated by Ostap Kin and Ali Kinsella

233

Notes

Dates of the poems are indicated, where known; otherwise, angle brackets, < >, are used to indicate the publication year of the collections the poems were included in.

Mykhail Semenko
"System" (p. 9)

Filippo Tommaso Marinetti (1876–1944) was an Italian poet, editor, and founder of the Futurist movement.

Constantin Guys (1802–1892) was a French realist painter and illustrator who was in contact with Baudelaire.

Umberto Boccioni (1882–1916) was an Italian painter and sculptor who shaped the Futurist movement.

Gérard de Nerval (1808–1855) was a French writer, poet, essayist and translator. He is one of the most important figures of French romanticism.

Panfuturism is a Ukrainian avant-garde movement initiated by Mykhail Semenko. In his article "What Panfuturism wants," Semenko outlines the main goals of this literary movement, and therefore Panfuturism "wants to be a scientific system which is attained by its being a system universal and synthetic"; "wants to abolish all 'isms'"; "is a revolutionary conception"; "is a proletarian system of art"; "changes the very substance of art and becomes an experimental science"; "is an organizational art"; "cannot be a 'new direction' in art"; "is the whole art and in the future — what will substitute it"; "is the system liquidating the old art in its pretension to be an active factor"; "is at once Futurism, Cubism, Expressionism and Dadaism, it is, however, no synthesis of these useful things"; "wants to be organizational ideologically"; "does not want to be utopia, but practice"; "is a practical system of the prolyterian art" (*Zwishen Stadt und Steppe: kunstlerische Texte der ukrainischen Moderne aus den 1910er bis 1930er Jahren*, Marina Dmitrieva, ed. [Berlin: Lucas, 2010], 256–257).

AS p/f Ukr. stands for the Association of Panfuturists in Ukraine (*Assotsiitsia panfuturystiv or Aspanfut*), a futurist literary group founded in Kyiv in November 1921 by Mykhail Semenko with Oleksa Slisarenko, Geo Shkurupiy,

Yulian Shpol and others. Its two emblematic publications included the jour-
nals *Semafor u maibutnie* [Semafor into the Future] and *Katafalk isskustva*
[Catafalque of Art]. At some point in the end of 1923 and/or in the begin-
ning of 1924, the group ceased to exist, with its founding members gradually
organizing and moving into new literary groups of that vibrant time.

Geo Shkurupiy (1903–1937) is a writer of poetry, prose, and one of the most
active members of Ukrainian futurist movement. He was also a dynamic
member of the Association of Panfuturists. The Futurist corpus of his own
texts is "one of the best and the largest," and "[t]hanks to a penchant for inno-
vation, an antipathy to lyricism, a deliberate engagement to political and liter-
ary polemics—Shkuripii's legacy stands as an apt and an ample example of the
[Futurist] movement's poetic practice" (Ilnytzkyj, *Ukrainian Futurism*, 263).

Kobzar is a poetry collection Semenko published in 1924; in addition, there is a
collection of poems entitled *Kobzar* (1840) by Taras Shevchenko. Semenko's ref-
erence to Shevchenko's *Kobzar*, a poetry collection considered by many scholars
to be an extremely vital example of Ukrainian poetry, goes as far back as to 1914
when the futurist poet, in the manifesto "Sam" (Alone), declared his willingness
and readiness to burn Shevchenko's *Kobzar*. It has been intended to have been
read and interpreted and understood as a symbolical act of cutting ties with the
traditionalist past, in Semenko's point of view. About ten years later, Semenko pub-
lished his first extensive volume of collected poems, over 600 pages, and gave it the
title *Kobzar*—a direct allusion to Shevhenko's earlier collection. It is also a hint that
the whole idea of naming a collection *Kobzar* was present in his mind back then.
For the analysis of the relationship between the futurists and the poet Shevchenko,
see the article by Oleh S. Ilnytzkyj [Oleh Ilnyts'kyi, "Shevchenko i futurysty,"
Suchasnist' No. 5 (1989)]. Finally, there is a famous cartoon by B. Frydkin entitled
"Kobzari [Shevchenko and Semenko]," in which Semenko says: "Move a bit, Taras
Hryhorovych, for we will be mixed up."
A *kobzar*, literally a "kobza player," is a bard who travelled in Ukraine in predom-
inantly XIX century and played and sung folkloric songs, often accompanied by
play on an instrument called *kobza*.

Yulian Shpol (real name, Mykhailo Yalovy; 1895–1937) was a poet, prose
writer, playwright and translator. In the early 1920s, he was one of the founders
of "*Udarna hrupa poetiv-futurystiv*" and until 1923, was closely affiliated with
the Ukrainian futurist movement. Afterwards, he was a member of literary

organizations Hart and Vaplite, both literary organizations that opposed the futurist literary declarations and visions.

Oleksa Slisarenko, see **Poets**

Drum — it could have possibly been an allusion to the forthcoming book by Oleksa Slisarenko, *Baraban. Vitryna druha* [Drum. The Second Display Window] (Kyiv: Panfuturysty, 1923).

9 poems is a collection of Mykhail Semenko's poems (Kyiv: Siaivo, 1918).

Panfuturists' October Anthology (in Ukrainian, *Zhovtnevyi zbirnyk panfuturystiv*) [Kyiv: Golfstrom, 1923] is a forty-page publication that contained Semenko's poem-mottos as well as typographic works by Geo Shkurupiy and Nik [Mykola] Bazhan (Anna Belaia and Andrei Rossomakhin, eds. *Mikhail' Semenko i ukrainskii panfuturizm: Manifesty. Mistifikatsiia. Stat'i. Lirika. Viziopoeziia* [St. Petersburg: Evropeiskii universitet v Sankt-Peterburge, 2016], 323).

Mykhail Semenko, see **Poets**

Mykola Bazhan (1904–1983) was a poet, writer, translator and Soviet Ukrainian political and cultural figure. At the time when Semenko published his poem (1922), Bazhan was an emerging poet as well as a cover designer who just recently moved from the province to the capital. Despite his young age, the poet was already recognized in the literary milieu of Ukrainian futurists for his outstanding talent. With the passing years, Bazhan's poetical lens drifted away from the futuristic aspirations of his youth but he nonetheless remained an important poet of his generation. He later became one of the most influential and widely recognized figures in the literary and cultural world of the Soviet Ukraine, in particular, and in the Soviet Union, in general.

"Steppe" is a poem Semenko published in 1919, shortly after the poem "Comrade Sun." The use of this one in "System" could have also been appre-hended as an early sign of poet's deliberations or play with a title for a future book, since the collection entitled *Step* [Steppe] indeed would have been published a few years after the poem "System" was written (Kyiv: Derzhavne vydavnytstvo Ukrainy, 1925). For the discussion of the 1919 poem "Steppe," see the critical essay by Borys Yakubsky (Borys Iakubs'kyi, "Mykhail' Semenko," *Chervonyi shliakh* 1–2 [1925]).

Com. Sun stands for "Comrade Sun," (Tov[arysh] Sontse, in Ukrainian) and is a "rev[olutionary]fut[uristic]poem" by Semenko that was published as a separate book (Kyiv, 1919).

Dmytro Zahul (1890–1944) was a poet-symbolist, literary scholar, and critic. In his 1922 article, Semenko criticized Zahul, and that very article coincides with the Semenko's writing of the poem "System," created in the same year. Zahul was chided for the fact that he "rehashed and translated Bal'mont while stumbling around Kyiv's cafes" (Anatol' Tsebro [Mykhail' Semenko], "Futuryzm v ukrains'kii poezii (1914–1922)" [Ilnytzkyj, *Ukrainian Futurism*, 33). Despite the critical approach to the futuristic movement, in the late 1920s Zahul positively responded to the launch of the journal *Nova generatsiia*, edited by Mykhail Semenko. In 1933, he was arrested and sentenced to ten years in the labor camps. He died in Kolyma in one of the camps.

Yakiv Savchenko (1890–1937) was a poet and literary critic. In the 1920s he worked at the newspapers *Bil'shovyk* and *Proletars'ka pravda*. During the 1910s he published various works, predominantly in the symbolist genre. He contributed to the journal *Mystetstvo* (Art), edited by Mykhail Semenko.

Pavlo Tychyna (1891–1967) was a poet, translator, and a high-ranking Soviet Ukrainian political and cultural figure. His output is considered to be an important contribution to Ukrainian symbolism. Semenko considered Tychyna to be his epigone, and believed that Tychyna's experimentation with words in his early poetry collections were based on Semenko's first two books (Belaia and Rossomakhin, *Mikhail' Semenko*, 341).

Quero-Futurism (*Kvero-futuryzm*) is a collection of Semenko's poems (1914). The collection comprised twenty-five poems poems and two manifestos. "Quero-Futurism" is also a 1914 manifesto in which the poet suggested that art is the constant process of seeking.

Oleksandr Oles (real name, Oleksandr Kandyba; 1878–1944) was a Ukrainian poet, writer, playwright and representative of the symbolism movement in

Ukrainian poetry. After the fall of the Ukrainian National Republic, Oles immigrated to the West and lived in the Czech Republic until the end of his life.

Prelude is the first collection of Semenko's poetry (Kyiv, 1913) that consisted of forty-one poems.

Mykola Vorony (1871–1938) was a poet, journalist, and theater director. Vorony, who is considered to be one of the first modernists in Ukrainian poetry, at the same time was criticized for his poetic output, which was believed to be somewhat limited in its scope, with a tendency toward repetition of the same themes.

Hrytsko Chuprynka (1879–1921) was a Modernist poet. A native of the Chernivih region, from 1910 he resided in Kyiv and published his work in the journal *Ukrains'ka khata*. An author of seven collections of poetry, and a three-volume collected poems, Chuprynka died under unknown circumstances.

"The Rest" (p. 11)

Vladivostok is a city in the Far East region of Russia. Semenko spent several years there in the 1910s when he was conscripted to serve in the army.

Khreshchatyk is the main street in the Ukrainian capital city of Kyiv. It has been a seminal locale in Ukrainian literature and especially vital for the Ukrainian futuristic poetry of the 1910s to the 1930s and, in general, throughout the twentieth century.

Reiterska Street is a street located not far from Khreshchatyk, in a central part of Kyiv.

V. Rudeychuk *"New York"* (p. 27)

West Broadway is a street in Manhattan.

Ivan Kulyk

From the poem "Black Epos" (p. 31)

Sambo is a character from a children's book *The Story of Little Black Sambo* (1899) by Helen Bannerman. In the mid-twentieth century, the book would be regarded as an object of racial allegations.

At Ypres and on the Marne is a reference to the First Battle of Ypres (Fall 1914) and the Second Battle of Ypres (April-May 1915), fights that took place for control of the strategic Flemish town of Ypres in western Belgium. The Battle of the Marne during World War I took place September 6–10, 1914.

Andriy Malyshko

"Mayakovsky in New York" (p. 87)

The Russian poet Vladimir Mayakovsky visited New York City in June 1925 while traveling in North America. On the first day of his stay in New York, Mayakovsky met with his old friend, David Burliuk. Mayakovsky spent a total of three months in the United States and, in addition to New York City, visited such cities as Detroit, Chicago, Cleveland, Philadelphia and Pittsburg. His corpus of texts—both poetry and prose—were later published to great success.

Yevhen Malanyuk

"New York Shorthand" (p. 43)

Mykhaylo Mukhyn (1894, Kyiv–1974, Algans, France) was a Ukrainian literary scholar, critic and essayist. After the fall of the Ukrainian National Republic, Mukhyn lived in the Czech Republic, and, following the Second World War, in the South of France. Like Malanyuk, during the interwar period Mukhyn cooperated with the *Visnyk*, a magazine whose editor-in-chief was Dmytro Dontsov.

Šumava, known in English predominantly as the Bohemian Forest, is a low mountain range in Central Europe, extending from the Czech Republic and Austria and Bavaria in Germany. Malanyuk lived in the Czech Republic after the fall the Ukrainian National Republic.

Solveig is a central character in the play "Peer Gynt" by Henrik Ibsen.
Yuriy Tarnawsky

The locales of the poems were supplied by the author.

"Ode to a Café" (p. 91)

The cafe in question is the original Pandora's Box, located at Bleecker Street at 7th Avenue in Greenwich Village, New York City.

Orest L. Voronevych was an artist born in Ukraine who moved to the United States after World War II. His work appeared in books published by members of the New York Group of Ukrainian poets. Voronevych designed the cover for the poetry collection *Life in a City* (1956) by Yuriy Tarnawsky.

"Sundays" (p. 95)

The places referred to are Newark, New Jersey and Manhattan, New York.

"Love Poem" (p. 99)

The place in question is 8th Street around Astor Place in Manhattan, New York.

"Arrival IV" (p. 101)

The place in question is the Wall Street and Battery Park area of the Lower Manhattan, New York.

Bohdan Boychuk

"City Verses" (p. 111)

Bleecker Street is a street in Manhattan located in Greenwich Village.

From *"Three Dimensional Love"* (p. 121)

Buchach is a town located on the Strypa River in the Ternopil oblast in Western Ukraine.

Strypa River is a river in Ternopil region in Western Ukraine.

"Luncheonette Triptych" (p. 127)

Varick Street is a street running in Lower Manhattan in New York City.

Borys Oliynyk

"New York Burns" (p. 157)

Hold on, hold on, was it not… on the cliffs of the Elbe—this is the poet's allusion to the encounter on the Elbe between the Soviet and American troops that occurred on April 25, 1945. It is the event that has usually been referred to in the West as "Elbe Day" and in the East, the "Encounter at the Elbe."

Yuri Andrukhovych

"Bombing New York City" (p. 181)

The Chrysler Building is a skyscraper located in Midtown Manhattan, at the intersection of 42nd Street and Lexington Avenue.

The Seagram Building is a skyscraper located in Midtown Manhattan, on Park Avenue between 52nd Street and 53rd Streets.

Vasyl Makhno

"New York Postcard to Bohdan Zadura" (p. 183)

Bohdan Zadura is a contemporary Polish poet and translator. In particular, he is a prolific translator of Ukrainian literature into Polish. Zadura, among other works, translated three collections of poems, one collection of essays, and one collection of short stories by Vasyl Makhno. Makhno, too, translated some of Zadura's poetry into Ukrainian.

Witold Gombrowicz (1904–1969) was a Polish writer and playwright.

Stanislaw Ignacy Witkacy (1895–1939) was a Polish writer, painter, philosopher, and novelist active in the interwar period.

Bruno Schulz (1892–1942) was a Polish Jewish writer, artist, and literary critic. He is regarded as one of the great Polish-language prose stylists of the twentieth century. The writer was born in the city of Drohobych, now Ukraine, where he spent his entire life and wrote his famous collections of prose.

Zbigniew Herbert (1924–1998) was a Polish poet, essayist, and drama writer. Born in Lviv, Herbert was forced out his native city and re-settled in Poland.

Magdeburg rights or laws were a set of town privileges first developed by Roman Emperor in tenth century, and regulated the degree of internal autonomy within cities and villages, granted by the local ruler.

Shmuel Agnon (1888–1970) was a Nobel Laureate and one of the central figures of modern Hebrew literature. He was born in the town of Buchach, in the Austro-Hungarian Empire (now Ukraine), and lived there until immigrating to Palestine in 1908. The town of Buchach regularly features in Agnon's fiction.

Ternopil is a regional center in Western Ukraine.

Pulawy is a Polish town where the poet Bohdan Zadura presently lives and works.

"Federico Garcia Lorca" (p. 193)

The Cotton Club was a club located in New York City in the Harlem neighborhood on 142nd Street and Lenox Avenue from 1923 to 1935. Later it operated in Midtown, in the Theater District.

"A Farewell to Brooklyn" (p. 197)

"Coney Island" is a 2006 play by Vasyl Makhno. For its English translation by Alexander Motyl, see Vasyl Makhno, "Coney Island: A Drama Operetta," *Ukrainian Literature*, Vol. 4 (2014): 187–202.

Flatbush is a neighborhood in the New York City borough of Brooklyn.

"Brooklyn Elegy" (p. 201)

Uman is a city in Central Ukraine. Every Rosh Hashana, Hassids from all over the world make the pilgrimage to the grave of Rabbi Nachman of Breslov.

"Staten Island" (p. 203)

Capodanno Boulevard is the short name of Father Capodanno Boulevard, which runs through several neighborhoods in the borough of Staten Island of New York City.

Iryna Vikyrchak

"To R.A." (p. 221)

Rose Ausländer is a Jewish German- and English-language poet born in the city of Chernivtsi/Czernowitz in the Bukowina part of the Austro-Hungarian Empire (now Ukraine). She lived in New York for some time, where she published a collection of poems originally written in English, although her main body of work was written in German. She later moved to Germany and lived in the town of Dusseldorf.

Oleksandr Fraze-Frazenko

"At Maikley Café" (p. 225)

Maikley Café is a place located in Brooklyn's Chinatown on Eighth Avenue.

Hrytsko Chubay (1949–1982) was a Ukrainian poet and one of the central figures in underground Ukrainian culture of Lviv. Chubay edited the *samizdat* journal *Skrynia* (The Chest). His first collection of poetry was published posthumously in 1990.

Oleh Lysheha (1949–2014) was a Ukrainian poet, essayist, translator and sculptor. He spent a year in the United States as a Fulbright Scholar. His collection *The Selected Poems* (1999), in the English translation by James Brasfield, was awarded the 2000 PEN Award for Poetry in Translation.

Ihor Kalynets (1939) is a Ukrainian poet and dissident belonging to the generation of *shestydesiatnyky* (the Sixties generation). His first collection appeared in 1960s in the Soviet Ukrainian, but later, due to censorship, his works were published predominantly in the West. A collection of his poems has appeared in English translation. Kalynets presently lives in Lviv.

Mr. Nobody is the title of a book by Ihor Kalynets as well as the name of the main character in the story.

Frederick Law Olmsted (1922–1903) was an American landscape architect, journalist, and social critic. He is considered to be the father of American landscape architecture.

Fujian is a province on the southeast coast of China. Brooklyn's Chinatown, established in the Sunset Park area of the New York City borough of Brooklyn, is known for being an enclave for Fuzhou immigrants from the Fujian Province.

Olha Fraze-Frazenko

"December" (p. 233)

In a few days we'll walk from Fulton Station to Fulton Station—meaning, most likely, the two stations: one in Manhattan and one in Brooklyn, New York. There also are two streets in New York called Fulton, also located in Manhattan and Brooklyn.

Acknowledgement of Publications in Ukrainian

"Cablepoem No. 2," "Cablepoem No. 6," "System," and "The Rest" by Mykhail Semenko are reprinted from Mykhail Semenko, *Kobzar* (Derzhavne vydavnytstvo Ukrainy, 1924).

"Walt Whitman" by Oleksa Slisarenko is reprinted from the literary journal *Chernovyi shliakh*, 1923.

"Subway" and "On Fifth Avenue" by Mykola Tarnovsky is reprinted from Mykola Tarnovs'kyi, *Do svitloi mety: Vybrani poezii* (New York: Liha Amerykans'kykh Ukraintsiv, 1951).

"In the City Where Walt Whitman Used to Live" by Mykola Tarnovsky is reprinted from Mykola Tarnovs'kyi, *Do svitloi mety: Vybrani poezii* (New York: Liha Amerykans'kykh Ukraintsiv, 1951).

"Times Square" by Kasandryn is reprinted from the journal *Smikh i pravda*, March 15, 1924.

"Enough" by M. Pilny is reprinted from the journal *Svitlo*, No. 2, December (1928).

"New York" by V. Rudeychuk is reprinted from journal *Svitlo*, No. 2, December (1928).

From the poem "Black Epos" is reprinted from Ivan Kulyk, *Virshi ta poemy* (Kyiv: Radians'kyi pys'mennyk, 1962).

"Mayakovsky in America" by Andriy Malyshko is reprinted from Andrii Malyshko, *Za synim morem* (Kyiv: Radians'kyi pys'mennyk, 1950).

"No, neither a desert, nor a tent…," "There are no mountains, there are no fields…," and "Thoughts" by Yevhen Malanyuk is reprinted from Ievhen Malaniuk, *Ostannia vesna* (New York: Vydannia "Visnyka," 1959).

"New York Shorthand" and "One Day" by Yevhen Malanyuk is reprinted from Ievhen Malaniuk, *Poezii* (New York: Naukove Tovarystvo im. Shevchenka i Ukrains'ka Vil'na Akademiia Nauk, 1954).

"Days" by Yevhen Malaniuk is reprinted from Ievhen Malaniuk, *Serpen'* (V-vo Niu-Iorks'koi Hrupy, 1964).

"New York Verses" by Vadym Lesych is reprinted from Vadym Lesych, *Rozmovy z bat'kom* (New York: Ob'iednannia Ukrains'kykh Pys'mennykiv "Slovo," 1957).

"Harlem" and "The Settled People" by Vadym Lesych is reprinted from Vadym Lesych, *Kreidiane kolo* (New York: Vydannia Na Hori, 1960).

"A Night on East Bronx" by Vadym Lesych is reprinted from Vadym Lesych, *Kam'iani luny* (New York: Vydannia Chotyriokh Svobid Ukrainy, 1964).

"Manhattan, 103rd Street" by Yuri Kosach is reprinted from Iurii Kosach, *Kubok Hanimeda: vybir poezii* (New York: Vydavnytstvo "Lesyn dim," 1958).

"Ballad of Golden Broadway" and "New York Elegy" by Yuri Kosach were reprinted from collection Iurii Kosach, *Vybrane: poezii, publitsystyka* (Kyiv: Dnipro, 1975).

"Broadway," "Diamond District," and "From the Song of Harlem" by Yuri Kosach are reprinted from Iurii Kosach, *Manhattans'ki nochi: balady, elehii, virshi* (Kyiv: Radians'kyi pys'mennyk, 1966).

"Ode to a Café" and "Sundays" by Yuriy Tarnawsky are reprinted from Iurii Tarnavs'kyi, *Zhyttia v misti* (New York: Ob'iednannia ukrains'kykh pys'mennykiv "Slovo," 1956).

"Love Poem" by Yuriy Tarnawsky is reprinted from Iurii Tarnavs'kyi, *Popoludni v Pokipsi* (New York: V-vo Niu-iorks'koi hrupy, 1960).

"Arrivals IV" by Yuriy Tarnawsky is reprinted from Iurii Tarnavs'kyi, *Bez Espanii* (Munich: Suchasnist', 1969).

"End of the World" by Yuriy Tarnawsky is reprinted from Iurii Tarnavs'kyi, *Os' iak ia vyduzhuiu* (Suchanist', 1978).

"Dddeath" by Yuriy Tarnawsky is reprinted from Iurii Tarnavs'kyi, *Ikh nemaie* (Kyiv: Rodovid, 1999).

"Homeless" by Bohdan Rubchak is reprinted from Bohdan Rubchak, *Kaminnyi sad* (New York: Ob'iednannia Ukrains'kykh Pys'mennykiv Slovo, 1956).

"A Negro Sits in the Middle of the Road and Beats a Drum" by Bohdan Boychuk is reprinted from the journal *Novi Poezii* 6 (1964).

"City Verses," "Letters," "Luncheonette Triptych," and from "Three Dimensional Love" by Bohdan Boychuk are reprinted from Bohdan Boichuk, *Virshi vybrani i peredostanni* (New York: Suchasnist', 1983).

"New York Elegy" by Bohdan Boychuk is reprinted from *Suchasnist'* 7–8 (1979).

"Autumn in Bronx Park" by Leonid Lyman is reprinted from the journal *Literaturno-naukovyi zbirnyk* 1 (1952).

"Broadway in the Evening" by Dima is reprinted from Dima, *Tretii bereh* (New York, 1963).

"New York at Night" by Dima is reprinted from Dima, *Osinnie merezhyvo* (New York, 1984).

"New York's Air" by Dmytro Pavlychko is reprinted from Dmytro Pavlychko, *Liubov i nenavyst'*, (Kyiv: Dnipro, 1975).

"Eternal Blues," "Two Walk in the Evening," "New York in the Cubist Style," and from "For Dmytro Pavlychko" by Ivan Drach are reprinted from Ivan

Drach, *Amerykans'kyi zoshyt: virshi, pereklady, dramatychna poema* (Kyiv: Molod', 1980).

"A Hot Day in New York" by Lida Palij is reprinted from Lida Palii, *Zhinka u vikni* (Ivano-Frankivs'k, 2001).

"From The White Home to the White House" by Borys Oliynyk is reprinted from Borys Oliinyk, *Shliakh* (Kyiv: Naukova dumka, 1978).

"Walt Street" and "On Broadway" by Abram Katsnelson are reprinted from Abram Katsnel'son, *Liryka* (Kyiv: Astarta, 2002).

"Bombing New York" by Yuri Andrukhovych is reprinted from Iurii Andrukhovych, *Pisni dlia mertvoho pivnia* (Ivano-Frankivs'k: Lileia-NV, 2004).

"New York Fuckin' City" by Serhiy Zhadan is reprinted from Serhii Zhadan, *Dynamo Kharkiv* (Kyiv: A-ba-ba-ha-la-ma-ha, 2014).

"And the smallest girl in Chinatown…" by Serhiy Zhadan is reprinted from Serhii Zhadan, *Efiopiia* (Kharkiv: Folio, 2009).

"New York Postcard to Bohdan Zadura" and "Coffee In Starbucks" by Vasyl Makhno are reprinted from Vasyl' Makhno, *38 virshiv pro Niu-Iork i deshcho inshe* (Kyiv: Krytyka, 2004).

"Federico Garcia Lorca" by Vasyl Makhno is reprinted from Vasyl' Makhno, *Cornelia Street Café: novi ta vybrani virshi, 1991–2006* (Kyiv: Fakt, 2007).

"A Farewell to Brooklyn," "Brooklyn Elegy" and "Staten Island" by Vasyl Makhno are reprinted from Vasyl' Makhno, *Zymovi lysty* (Kyiv: Krytyka, 2011).

"Eleventh Street" by Maryana Savka is reprinted from Mar'iana Savka, *Boston-dzhaz* (Kyiv: Fakt, 2008).

"My friend Stefan in corduroy jacket …" by Oksana Lutsyshyna is reprinted from a manuscript received from the author.

"Painkillers and Sleeping Pills" by Kateryna Babkina is reprinted from a manuscript received from the author.

"Big Fish and Other Things" by Iryna Shuvalova is reprinted from a manuscript received from the author.

"R.A." and "Seasonal" by Iryna Vikyrchak are reprinted from the manuscripts received from the author.

"At Maikley's Café" by Oleksandr Fraze-Frazenko is reprinted from a manuscript received from the author.

"'In tunnels of white tiles yellow fish are cruising'…" by Yulia Musakovska is reprinted from a manuscript received from the author.

"New York" by Vasyl Lozynsky is reprinted from publication in *Hawai'i Review* 86 Spring (2017).

"December" by Olha Fraze-Frazenko is reprinted from a manuscript received from the author.

Prior Publications in English Translation

Kateryna Babkina: "Painkillers and Sleeping Pills" appeared in *Kenyon Review* Vol. XXXVIII, No. 2 March-April (2016).

Bohdan Boychuk: "Letters" as well as "Three" and "Eleven" from "Three Dimensional Love" appeared in Bohdan Boychuk, *Memories of Love* (Riverdale-on-Hudson, NY: Sheep Meadow Press, 1989).

Vasyl Lozynsky: "New York" appeared in *Hawai'i Review* 86 (Spring 2017).

Vasyl Makhno: "Federico Garcia Lorca" and "A Farewell to Brooklyn" appeared in Vasyl Makhno, *Thread and Selected New York Poems* (New York: Meeting Eyes Bindery, 2009).

_____. "Brooklyn Elegy" and "Staten Island" appeared in Vasyl Makhno, *Winter Letters and Other Poems* (New York: Spuyten Duyvil, 2011).

_____. "Coffee in Starbucks" appeared in *Poetry International Web* 2005.

_____. "New York Postcard to Bohdan Zadura" appeared in *DeKadentzya*, vol. 2 (2010).

Yuriy Tarnawsky: "End of the World" appeared in Iurii Tarnav'skyi, *Os' iak ia vyduzhuiu* [=*This is how I get well*] (Suchasnist', 1970).

Serhiy Zhadan: ["And the smallest little girl in Chinatown"] appeared in *The Common* (October 2015).

Artists

David Burliuk (1882–1967) was a Futurist author and theoretician associated with Russian Futurism. Born in Kharkiv Governorate of the Russian Empire (what is now the Sumy region in Ukraine), the poet and artist was an influential figure in the Russian avant-garde movement of the 1910s and early 1920s. In the 1920s he immigrated from the Soviet Union and soon landed in the United States, where he continued his active work as an artist and author, and published, among other things, numerous collections of materials related to the Futurism.

Kateryna Krychevska-Rosandich (1926, Kyiv), an artist, was influenced by her family. She studied at an art school in Kyiv before the war, and at the Industrial Art School in Prague during the war. In 1949 she moved to the United States. Her works are held in the museum and private collections in Ukraine, the United States, and Canada. She lives in Mountain View, California.

Abram Manievich (1891, Mstyslav, Belarus–1942, New York) was born in Mstyslav, now Belarus, studied in Kyiv Art College in 1901–1905, in the Academy of Art in 1905–1906 in Munich, and later taught at the Kyiv Academy of Art. In 1921, the artist immigrated to the United States, settled in the Bronx and was critically acclaimed until his death. The artist is most known for his works belonging to the Kyiv period as well as to New York period.

Zenowij Onyshkewych (1929, Lviv) is a post-war émigré artist. He studied at the Art Students' League of New York, the National Academy of Fine Arts, and the Pratt Institute. From 1977 to 1984, he taught drawing at Fairfield University. *The New York Times, Reader's Digest,* and various other American publishing houses featured his illustrations. Solo exhibitions of his work have been held in New York, Washighton, Chicago, Rome, Toronto, with his latest exhibition in the Ukrainian Museum in New York in 2016. He lives in Connecticut.

Arcadia Olenska-Petryshyn (1934, Roznoshentsi, now Ukraine–1996, New Brunswick, NJ), painter and critic, since 1950 lived in the United States. In 1955, she received a Bachelor's degree from Hunter College, and an MFA from the University in Chicago in 1963. The bulk of her work comprises lithographs, graphics, and oil works. Her oeuvre, in general, might be divided into abstracts works, paintings of cacti, and prints of plants and trees. She had solo exhibits in New York, Chicago, Toronto, Edmonton, Antwerp, Brussels, Shenyang, Lviv, Kyiv and elsewhere. She also served as an art editor of the journal *Suchasnist*.

Myroslav Radysh (1910, Ilyntsi, Sniatyn county, Galicia–1956, New York), a painter and scenery designer, graduated from the Poznan Art School. In post-war period, he worked as an artist and scenery designer in Augsburg, Germany. After moving to New York in 1950, Radysh taught art and participated in several solo and group exhibitions in New York and Philadelphia. A catalogue of Radysh's work entitled *Radysh* (1966) was published posthumously.

Mikhail Turovsky (1933, Kyiv) graduated from Kyiv Art Institute in 1965 and continued his postgraduate studies at the Moscow Academy of Art until 1968. He immigrated with his family to the United States in 1979. His works has been exhibited in New York, Jerusalem, Paris, Brussels, Madrid, Venice, among others. In 2009 the exhibition of the Turovsky Holocaust painting was held at the Headquarters of the United Nations in New York. His works are part of permanent collections at the National Art Museum in Kyiv, the State Tretyakov Gallery in Moscow, the Yad Vashem Memorial Art Museum in Jerusalem, and in other public and private collection. In 2008 he was awarded the title of People's Artist of Ukraine.

Anton Varga (1989) is a founding member of the Open Group, an initiative of young artists formed in the city of Lviv in 2012. He studied at Zakarpattia Art Institute and Kharkiv State Academy of Arts and Design. As a member of the Open Group, he has received various awards and shown his work in exhibitions such as the Venice Biennale. He lives and works in New York.

Poets

Yuri Andrukhovych (1960, Ivano-Frankivsk) is poet, prose writer, essay-ist, and translator. In addition to several collections of poetry and essays, Andrukhovych authored five novels: *Recreation* (1990, English translation, 2000), *The Moscoviad* (1992, English translation, 2012), *Perverzion* (1997, English translation, 2005), *Twelve Rings* (2004, English translation, 2015). A collection of selected essays, *My Final Territory* (2018), was published by the University of Toronto Press. A recipient of several literary awards, including the Hannah Arend Prize (2015), Andrukhovych lives in Ivano-Frankivsk.

Kateryna Babkina (1985, Ivano-Frankivsk) is a poet and prose writer, author of the poetry collections *St. Elmo's Fire* (2002), *The Mustard* (2011), and *Painkillers and Sleeping Pills* (2014); the short story collection *Leloo After You* (2008); as well as a novel titled *Sonya* (2013). The play *Hamlet-Babylon* was recently staged in Kyiv and Geneva. Her poetry and prose have been trans-lated and published in various collections and magazines in Poland, Germany, Russia, Sweden, Romania, France, and the United States. Babkina lives in Kyiv.

Bohdan Boychuk (1927, Bertnyky, Galicia–2017, Kyiv) was a poet, prose writer, translator, literary critic, and editor. He published many collections of poetry, prose, and translation. He compiled a two-volume anthology of Ukrainian poetry Koordynaty (Coordinates, 1969). A collection of his poetry, *Memories of Love*, appeared in English translation in 1989. Boychuk moved to the United States in 1949 and from the 1990s until his death resided in Kyiv.

Dima (real name, Diamara Khodymchuk; 1925, Romny, Poltava guberny) is a poet, actress, and prose writer. From 1945 she lived in Paris and worked in a theatre. In 1959 she moved to New York. She published six collections of poetry, prose, and poetry for children, as well as plays and essays.

Ivan Drach (1936, Telizhyntsi, Kyiv region–2018, Kyiv) is a poet, literary critic, translator, screenwriter, and political leader. An author of many crit-ically acclaimed collections of poetry, non-fiction, and scripts, in the 1980s he emerged as a political activist. A collection of his selected poetry, *Orchard Lamps*, edited by Stanley Kunitz, was published in English translation in 1978.

A collection of poems about his experience in the United States, *Amerykans'kyi zoshyt* (*American Notebook*), was published in 1980. He was awarded the highest literary awards in the Soviet Ukraine.

Oleksandr Fraze-Frazenko (1989, Lviv) is a filmmaker, poet, photographer, translator, musician and co-founder of "OFF Laboratory" production studio. He directed the documentaries *Chubay* (2014), *The House on Seven Winds* (2015), and *An Aquarium in the Sea* (2016). His first feature film, *Don't Lie to Me*, was presented in 2016. He has authored ten collection of poetry and translated the first poetry book of Jim Morrison in Ukraine.

Olha Fraze-Frazenko (1986, Lviv) is a film director, poet, and artist. She has authored two collections of poetry, *Museum of Toys* (2013) and *The Name of Water* (2017); directed a short film, *The Name of Water* (2015), and a feature documentary film, *I See* (2015). She is a co-founder and a CEO of OFF Laboratory Production Studio. Olha Fraze-Frazenko lives in Lviv.

Kasandryn (real name, Mykhaylo Andriychuk; 1894, Honchariv, Galicia–1938, New York) is a writer, editor, and civil activist. He moved to the United States in 1911. Known chiefly by his pen name M. Han, he worked as an editor-in-chief of the newspapers *Ukrains'ki visti* [The Ukrainian News] and *Robitnyk* [The Worker]. He was closely affiliated first with the Ukrainian Federation of the Socialist Party of the United States, and then, from 1919, with the Communist Party of the United States.

Abram Katsnelson (1914, Horodnia, Chernihiv gubernia–2003, Los Angeles) was a poet and literary critic. His first collection of poetry was published in 1937. He authored many poetry collections and collection of essays during the Soviet era. In August 1994 Katsnelson moved to the United States and lived in Los Angeles. After moving to the United States, he published three collections of poetry. His essays range thematically from poetry studies to analysis of poetic languages.

Yuri Kosach (1909, Kyiv–1989, Passaic, New Jersey) was a poet, writer, and playwright. He studied in Warsaw and Paris. After coming to the United States in 1949, he published the journal *Za synim obriem*. He was an extremely prolific and well-published author, both during his life in Europe and after immigration to the United States. From the 1960s to the 1980s, his collections of poetry were published both in the United States and in the Soviet Union, in what was an extremely unusual case. This was in addition's to the author's travel to the Soviet Ukraine.

Ivan Kulyk (born Yisroel ben Yehuda Kulyk; 1897, Shpola, Kyiv gubernia–1937, Kyiv) was a writer and political figure. In 1914, he emigrated to Pennsylvania and in 1917 returned to Ukraine. From 1924 to 1927, Kulyk was a Soviet consul in Montreal. He wrote over ten volumes of poetry and prose, and edited and translated *Antolohiia amerykans'koi poezii. 1855–1925* (Anthology of American Poetry, 1855–1925; 1928). In 1937, Kulyk was arrested and soon executed. In the 1960s, he was rehabilitated, and collections of his selected works were soon published.

Vadym Lesych (1909, Sniatyn, Galicia–1982, New York) was a poet and essayist. In Lviv, he published three collections of poetry in 1930s, and then stopped publishing his work for almost two decades. After moving to the United States in the late 1940s, Lesych published many collections of poetry. Lesych also authored a monograph on the artist Nykyfor, was a member of the PEN International organization.

Vasyl Lozynsky (1982, Lviv) is a Ukrainian poet, essayist, translator, literary critic, and curator. He published a chapbook *Feast after Debauchery* (2014) and a collection of poems *Another Country* (2016). Collection of his selected poems *Das Fest nach dem Untergang* appeared in German translation (2016). Lozynsky has translated Franz Kafka's and Ron Winkler's works, and edited and translated Tadeusz Dąbrowski's collection *Black Square* (2013). Lozynsky lives and works in Kyiv.

Oksana Lutsyshyna (1974, Uzhhorod) is a poet, fiction writer, and translator. She has authored two novels, a collection of short stories, and three collections of poetry. She also holds a PhD in comparative literature from the University of Georgia in the United States. Lutsyshyna currently is a lecturer in Ukrainian studies at the University of Texas at Austin.

Leonid Lyman (1922, Mali Sorochyntsi, Poltava gubernia–2003, New York) was a poet and prose writer. He immigrated to the United States and settled in New York in 1949. There he contributed to several Ukrainian newspapers as editor. In 1960s and 1970s, he was a founding editor of the sporadically published literary journal *Notatnyk*. In 2002, his first collection of poetry and prose, *Pam'iat'* (*Memory),* was published in Ukraine. He worked as an editor at various Ukrainian newspapers for most of his life spent in the US.

Vasyl Makhno (1964, Chortkiv, Ternopil region) is a poet, prose writer, essayist, and translator. He has authored ten collections of poetry, two books of essays, two plays, and a collection of short stories, *The House in Baiting Hollow* (2015). Two poetry collections, *Thread and Other New York Poems* (2009), *Winter Letters* (2011) and *Jerusalem Poems* (2016), were published in English translation. He is the 2013 recipient of Serbia's Povele Morave Prize in Poetry and the 2015 "BBC Book of the Year" award. Makhno lives in New York City.

Yevhen Malanyuk (1897, Novoarkhanhelsk, Kherson gubernia–1968, New York) was a poet and essayist. After the fall of the Ukrainian National Republic, he emigrated to Czechoslovakia. At the end of World War II, he resettled in Germany and later immigrated to the United States. His first collections of poetry appeared in Ukraine in the 1920s, and he continued to publish many more collections of poetry and essays in the United States. Several collections of his annotated poetry and memoirs have appeared in Ukraine after 1991.

Andriy Malyshko (1912, Obukhiv, Kyiv gubernia–1970, Kyiv) was a poet and publicist. During his lifetime, he authored numerous collections of poetry. His oeuvre also consists of collections of essays and translations from the Russian. Compilations of his works appeared at first in five volumes (1962), and later in ten volumes (1972–1974). He was also awarded various Soviet awards, including the Stalin Literary Award (1950).

Yulia Musakovska (1982, Lviv) is a poet and translator. She authored four collections of poetry: *On the Exhale and the Inhale* (2010), *Masks* (2011), *The Hunt for Silence* (2014) and *Men, Women and Children* (2011). In 2010 she was awarded the Smoloskyp literary prize. A translator of the poetry of Trastromer into Ukrainian and of Ukrainian poetry into English, her own poems have been translated into English, Polish, Bulgarian, German, and Hebrew. Musakovska lives in Lviv.

Borys Oliynyk (1935, Zachepylivka, Poltava oblast–2017, Kyiv) was a poet and Soviet and Ukrainian government official. In 1958 he graduated from Kyiv

University with a degree in journalism. He became active in administration of the Writers' Union of the USSR. His collections have been published since the early 1960s. In 1983, a collection of essays, *Planeta Poeziia* (The Planet Poetry), was published and in 1985, a two-volume compilation, *Vybrani tvory* (Selected Work), was published.

Lydia Palij (1926, Stryi, Galicia) is a poet, prose writer, and translator. During World War II she moved to the West, after spending a few years in displaced persons camps, and eventually immigrated to Canada, where she settled down in Toronto. She published a several collections of poetry and short stories, including one poetry collection in English. Palij was affiliated with the Canadian faction of the PEN Writers' Organization and was the last President of the Ukrainian Writers' Organization in Exile "Slovo." Palij lives in Toronto.

Dmytro Pavlychko (1929, Stopchativ, Ivano-Frankivsk oblast) is a poet, translator, and activist. In the Soviet era, Pavlychko was considered one of most widely recognized Soviet Ukrainian poets and received the highest literary awards. From 1971 to 1978 he was editor-in-chief of the journal *Vsesvit*. Over twenty volumes of his works were published from the 1950s to the 2010s. His collection of selected poetry in English translation, *Two Colors of Love*, was published in 2013. Pavlychko presently lives in Kyiv.

M. Pilny (real name, Leon Tolopko; 1902, New York–1991, New York) was a poet, writer, and civic activist. Born in the United States to parents who emigrated from Galicia, Pilny returned in early 1920s to Galicia, and taught at a local college. Shortly thereafter, Pilny returned to New York in the mid-1920s. Pilny co-authored two books about the life of Ukrainian workers in the United States and published them under his real name, Leon Tolopko. In the 1960s, he was editor-in-chief of the *Ukrains'ki Visti*, a Ukrainian New York-based daily newspaper.

Bohdan Rubchak (1935, Kalush, Galicia–2018, Boonton, New Jersey) is a poet, prose writer, and literary scholar. In 1948, Rubchak settled in the United States. In 1977, he defended his PhD dissertation in comparative literature at Rutgers University and later became professor of literature at the University of Illinois. He published five collections of poetry from the 1960s to the 1980s and numerous essays, in Ukrainian and English, on Ukrainian literature. With Bohdan Boychuk, he co-edited the two-volume anthology of contemporary Ukrainian poetry *Koordynaty* (Coordinates, 1969).

It is unclear if **V. Rudeychuk** is a real name or a pen name.

Maryana Savka (1973, Kopychyntsi, Ternopil region) is a poet, writer, and publisher. She has published around ten collections of poetry including *Boston Jazz* (2008), children books, and a monograph about the Ukrainian émigré press in Czechoslovakia. A collection of poetry, *Eight Notes from the Blue Angel*, appeared in English translated in limited edition (2007). She runs the Old Lion Publishing House and lives in Lviv.

Mykhail Semenko (1892, Kybyntsi, Poltava gubernia–1937, Kyiv) was a poet and theoretician of Ukrainian futurism. The author of numerous collections of poetry and prose, a complete edition of his work was published in three volumes in 1929 to 1931. In 1937, Semenko was arrested and executed. In the 1960s, he was rehabilitated.

Iryna Shuvalova (1986, Kyiv) is a poet and translator. She holds an MA degree in Comparative Literature from Dartmouth College and is presently a PhD candidate at the Slavic department at Cambridge University. She published three collections of poetry, *Ran* (2011), *Os* (2014), and *Az* (2014), and co-edited the first anthology of queer writing in Ukraine, *120 pages of Sodom* (2009). In 2011, she was the recipient of the Joseph Brodsky/Stephen Spender Prize for translation. She currently lives in Cambridge, United Kingdom.

Oleksa Slisarenko (real name, Oleksa Snisar; 1891, Konivtsov, Kharkiv gubernia–1937, Sandarmokh, Karelia region, RFSSR) was a poet and prose writer. He was co-editor of *Universal'nyi zhurnal* (1928–1929) and was a member of the Panfuturist organizations Association of Panfuturists and Komunkult as well as Hart and VAPLITE. Slisarenko published collections of poems *Poemy* (1923) and *Baida* (1928), a complete six-volume edition of his works was published in 1931–1933. Slisarenko was repressed during the Stalinist era because of his ties with the symbolists and Panfuturists, and was subsequently arrested in 1934 and sent to the Solovets Islands, where he was executed.

Yuriy Tarnawsky (1934, Turka, Sambir county, Galicia) is a poet, prose writer, translator, linguist and one of the founding member of the New York Group of poets well as one of the original Fiction Collective authors. He is the author of more than two dozens of books of fiction, poetry, drama, and translations. He holds a PhD in Linguistics from New York University and worked as a computer scientist at IBM Corporation, as well as professor of Ukrainian literature and culture at Columbia University.

Mykola Tarnovsky (1895, Kotsubyntsi, Galicia–1984, Lviv) is a poet, prose writer, translator. Author of many collections of poetry and prose, Tarnovsky came to the United States in 1917. In the 1920s, he edited leftist Ukrainian newspapers and journals and was involved with the Socialist organizations. In 1958, Tarnovsky returned to Soviet Ukraine. Until his death, Tarnovsky was a deputy chief at the Tovarytsvo Ukraina, an official Kyiv-based Soviet Ukrainian organization responsible for maintaining cultural bonds with the Ukrainian diaspora in the world.

Iryna Vikyrchak (1988, Zalishchyky, Ternopil region) is an author, cultural manager, and literature promoter. She has published two collections of poetry. She is the founder of the Intermezzo Short Story Festival in Vinnytsia and former director of the International Literature Corporation "Meridian Czernowitz" (the festival, publishing house, and residency for European poets in Chernivtsi). She is a PhD candidate in literature at Chernivtsi National Yuri Fedkovych University.

Oksana Zabuzhko (1960, Lutsk) is poet, prose writer, essayist and scholar. Her works translated into English include a collection of poems and essays *A Kingdom of Fallen Statues*, as well as the novels *Field Work in Ukrainian Sex* and *The Museum of Abandoned Secrets* (2012). Among her numerous acknowledgments are the Global Commitment Foundation Poetry Prize (1997), MacArthur Grant (2002), Antonovych International Foundation Prize (2008), the Ukrainian National Award, the Order of Princess Olha (2009), Angelus (2013), and many other national awards. Zabuzhko lives in Kyiv.

Serhiy Zhadan (1974, Starobilsk, Luhansk region) is poet, prose writer, essayist, and translator. He has authored two dozen collections of poetry, fiction, non-fiction, and translations. His two novels, *Depeche Mode* and *Voroshylovhrad*, appeared in English translation in 2013 and 2016, respectively, and a collection of short stories and poems, *Mesopotamia*, in 2018 from Yale University Press. His poetry and prose haven been featured in various American literary journals, both in print and online. A recipient of the Jan Michalski Prize for Literature (2014) and Angelus (2015), Zhadan lives and works in Kharkiv.

Translators

Bohdan Boychuk, see Poets

Marlow Davis is a PhD candidate in the Department of Slavic Languages and Literatures at Columbia University in the City of New York, where he is writing a dissertation on the auto-documentary writings of Iraida Kedrina Barry. His research focuses on the aesthetics and poetics of the 1910s and 1920s in Russian and Ukrainian literature and art. Davis received BA (2010), MA (2015), and MPhil (2017) degrees from Columbia University.

Anand Dibble is a poet and translator from the Ukrainian and Russian. He studied Russian literature at Hampshire College and lived for four years in Kyiv. His translations of Sergey Rudakov have appeared in the anthology *Written in the Dark: Five Poets in the Siege of Leningrad*, and his original writing has appeared in the *Ampersand Review*. He is currently working on a PhD in Slavic languages and literature at Stanford University.

Abbey Fenbert is a writer from Detroit. She holds an MFA in Playwriting from Boston University and a BA from NYU. Her original plays have been produced and developed by the Boston Playwrights' Theatre, Matrix Theatre Company, the Boston Theater Marathon, the KNOW Theatre, the Vagrancy and the Berkshire Playwrights Lab. Fenbert is currently based in Los Angeles, where she is Literary Manager of the Vagrancy Theatre Company.

Oleksandr Fraze-Frazenko, see Poets

Luba Gawur is a poet and translator. Born in Ohio, she completed studies in Slavic languages at Kent State University and the University of Toronto, and obtained an M.A. in library science. She has lived in Toronto, New York, Prague and Kyiv, and currently resides in Kent, Ohio. Her poetry and translations have been published in numerous journals and periodicals.

Olga Gerasymiv is an interdisciplinary artist, translator, and performer. She graduated from the Massachusetts College of Art and Design in 2010 with a double degree in Studio for Interrelated Media and Art History. She began translating Ukrainian poetry in 2014. Her translations of poetry have appeared in various anthologies. Other projects include video art, graphic design, and painting. Born in Lviv, Gerasymiv currently resides in Boston, MA.

Olena Jennings's collection of poetry *Songs from an Apartment* was published in January 2017 by Underground Books. Her translations of poetry from the Ukrainian can be found in *Chelsea*, *Poetry International*, and *Wolf*. She has published fiction in *Joyland*, *Pioneertown*, and *Projectile*. She completed her MFA in writing at Columbia and her MA focusing on Ukrainian literature at the University of Alberta.

Ali Kinsella has been translating from Ukrainian for five years. She holds a master's degree in Ukrainian Studies from Columbia University. She currently lives in Chicago, where she also sometimes works as a baker.

Jazlyn Kraft is a poet, essayist, and student of literature with an undergraduate degree in English and Philosophy from Hampshire College. When she is not rearranging her own words, she particularly enjoys editing for others.

Oksana Lutsyshyna, see Poets

Alexander J. Motyl is a writer, painter, and professor. Nominated for the Pushcart Prize in 2008 and 2013, he is the author of nine novels and one collection of poetry. His artwork has been shown in solo and group shows in New York, Philadelphia, Westport, and Toronto, and is part of the permanent collection of the Ukrainian Museum in New York and the Ukrainian Cultural Centre in Winnipeg. His paintings are on display on his website, www.alexmotyl.com. He teaches political science at Rutgers University-Newark and is the author of seven academic books and numerous articles.

Michael Naydan is the Woskob Family Professor of Ukrainian Studies at the Pennsylvania State University. He has published over forty articles on literary topics and more than seventy translations in journals and anthologies. His most recent books of translations include Andrei Sinyavsky's *Strolls with Pushkin* (2016) and Igor Klekh's *Adventures in the Slavic Kitchen: A Book of Essays with Recipes* (2016), both co-translated with Slava Yastremski, as well as Yuri Vynnychuk's *The Fantastic Worlds of Yuri Vynnychuk* (2016).

Wanda Phipps is the author of the books *Field of Wanting: Poems of Desire* and *Wake-Up Calls: 66 Morning Poems*. She received a New York Foundation for the Arts Poetry Fellowship. Her poems have appeared in over one hundred literary magazines and numerous anthologies. She has worked with Virlana Tkacz on translating Ukrainian poetry since 1989.

Orest Popovych is a professor emeritus at Brooklyn College of the City University of New York and former President of the Shevchenko Scientific Society (New York, NY). He has translated Vasyl Makhno's poetry collections "Thread and Selected New York Poems" (2009), "Winter Letters and Other Poems" (2011) and "Jerusalem Poems" (2016). For the first collection, he was awarded the AAUS 2010 Prize for Best Translation from Ukrainian.

Mark Rudman is a poet. He has taught at Columbia University and New York University and edited the literary magazine *Pequod*. An author of many collections of poetry and non-fiction, he has also translated, with Paul Nemser and Bohdan Boychuk, Bohdan Ihor Antonych's poetry collection *Square of Angels* (1977) and, with David Ignatow, Bohdan Boychuk's collection *Memories of Love* (1989). He lives in New York.

Yuriy Tarnawsky, see Poets

Virlana Tkacz is the artistic director of Yara Arts Group, a resident theatre company at La MaMa Experimental Theatre in New York. She has created over thirty shows with poetry she helped translate from Ukraine, Central Asia, and Siberia. She received an NEA Poetry Translation Fellowship for her translations with Wanda Phipps of Serhiy Zhadan. Her translation of Serhiy Zhadan's poetry collection is forthcoming with Yale University Press (2018).

Illustrations

Abram Manievich, "The Bronx" (1924). Reproduced with permission from the New York Historical Society.

David Burliuk, "Harlem River" (1924). Reproduced with permission from Mary Burliuk Holt.

Kateryna Krychevska-Rosandich, "New York" (1955). Reproduced with permission from Kateryna Krychevska Rosandich.

Myroslav Radysh, "Harbor" (ca. 1949-1956). Printed with the permission of Ihor Radysh and the Ukrainian Museum (New York).

Zenowij Onyshkewych, "New York in the 1960s" (1962). Reproduced with permission from Zenowij Onyshkewych.

Arcadia Olenska-Petryshyn, "Dwellings I" (1958). Reproduced with permission from Walter Petryshyn.

Mikhail Turovsky, "Cityscape, New York" (2006). Reproduced with permission from Mikhail Turovsky.

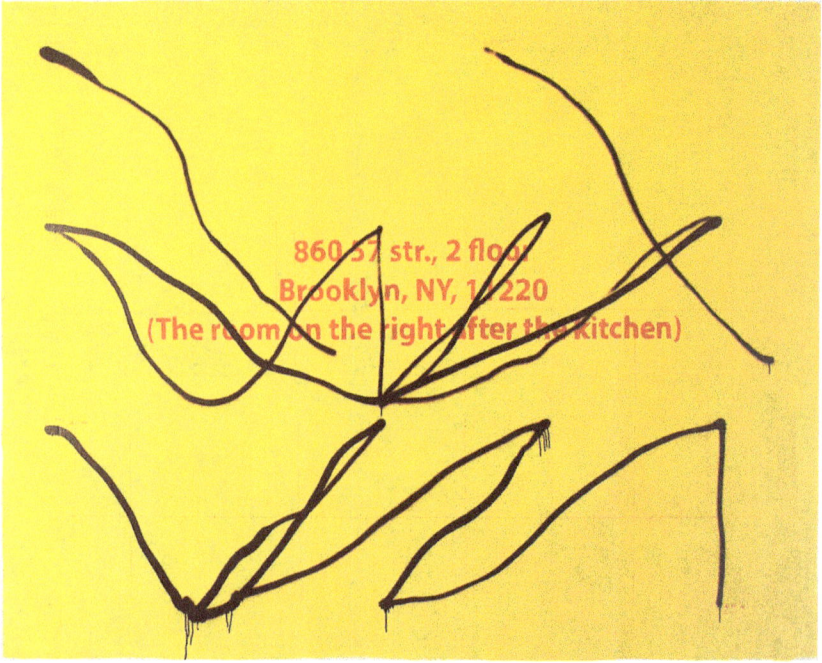

Anton Varga, "Untitled practice. Part 6.3" (2017). Reproduced with permission from Anton Varga.

Index of First Lines and Titles in Ukrainian

Titles appear in italics. If the title and the first line are identical, only the title is included.

The original titles in English are included in the end.

Index of First Lines and Titles in English

Titles appear in italics. When the first line equals the title, only the title is included.

Index

www.ingramcontent.com/pod-product-compliance
Lightning Source LLC
Chambersburg PA
CBHW061514020726
47502CB00006B/2074